MARK WOOD

SOLO EXPLORER

MARK WOOD

SOLO EXPLORER

WORDS by DESIGN

Mark would struggle with me describing his work as extraordinary, his modesty in talking about his own feats is humbling. Through the diary entries he kept on his solo expeditions to both the North and South Poles, we are treated to a stunning book that will transport us all to the breath-taking parts of the world Mark has called home for months at a time. As he moves through the endless ice we form an understanding of what made him give up everything to dedicate his time to a new way of life.

In my work over the years I have calculated risk constantly in pursuit of my own goals and when the odds are against you, your experience, training and knowledge will assist you. These attributes, coupled with the persistence that is ingrained within you, are what make our pursuits possible. Mark will tell you that one doesn't work without the other – that's when the extraordinary happens.

I understand the enormity of committing to a task that most people would consider impossible, how you can be successful when armed with a clear understanding of your own skills and how to react in adversity – whether that's under immense pressure against the clock or with time on your side. Your ability to make decisions is crucial in survival and Mark has encountered more moments of uncertainty than most of us can imagine, but he has always succeeded in pre-empting any high-risk scenario, however statistically unlikely, that can occur when you plunge yourself into the unknown.

Whether it's in business surrounded by home-comforts or out in the most extreme elements, when you find yourself at the centre of a storm it's down to how you respond as an individual. Your DNA, your ego, your belief in how you *make steps to improve the situation are what become the ultimate deciding factors in how you move forward, how you survive. The settings are remote areas around the world and the journeys are unique but the real story is how an individual can step away from what we perceive as 'normal life' to focus on his passion.*

Mountains, ice, deserts, jungles and seas are just platforms to operate in, but if we can take something from Mark's philosophy, it's that what you do in these remarkable parts of the planet can, will and do inspire. Mark recognises the love for all things exploration but also understands his own place within this, using his expeditions to reach out to younger generations and creating a buzz so that students can be a part of his experiences, regardless of their background, social status or geographical location. Through advancing technology and Mark's will to communicate from the most isolated parts of the globe, the barriers can be removed.

I have known Mark for many years and he is incredibly open and honest when talking about his vision. What's also apparent is his acceptance of vulnerability, being unafraid to ask questions or speak to other people to ascertain whether his vision is good enough. If you asked him what he thought success was, then it certainly wouldn't be based on how wealthy he is — success instead would be measured in fulfilment of his work.

Mark told me once that waving a flag on top of a mountain wasn't his reason for exploring. Instead, reaching out to students globally, speaking to prominent industry insiders about leadership tactics and candidly documenting his ventures are his motivation.

Mark is a patron of my charity Hire a Hero UK – an organisation that supports ex-military personnel in finding work and with their sometimes difficult transition back into civilian life. Mark's sense of moving forward with life, and the respect he asks for from the students and companies with which he works, is a clear reflection on our own ethos – respect yourself and take time to re-focus.

Solo Explorer isn't purely an account of one man's footsteps through an expedition. In one of the most unique books on exploration to date, Mark takes us to a place of fear and compassion. He shows curiosity for a bigger understanding of the world we live in, the footprints we're leaving, and a drive to inspire and influence change. This is a book that explores the extremes and reveals the human side to following your own passion in life – it's an honest read that offers an uninhibited and, at times, vulnerable view of what it takes to find yourself completely alone on the planet.

After closing the back page, I was left with the overwhelming feeling that we are only on the first chapter of a much bigger story.

Gerry Hill MBE QGM and Bar.
45 years in the British Army, 34 of which were served in
22 Special Air Service Regiment, now CEO of Hire a Hero UK

*Many years ago as a child I sat with you on my bed
and we looked out of the window together at the night stars.*

*We explored the universe in our very own make-believe spaceship.
Now I am older and as I walk into our planet's extremes,
I feel you with me, always.*

For my Mum.

Contents

In 1969, three years after I was born, astronaut Michael Collins sat silently in the Apollo 11 command module orbiting the moon over 200,000 miles away from earth.

He patiently waited within his capsule for a signal from NASA back on earth to begin the procedure for picking up his fellow astronauts, Neil Armstrong and Buzz Aldrin, from the moon's surface.

At that moment in time he was the most remote human being in the history of humanity – in total isolation, spinning above the surface of the moon, around to the dark side where light and all conception of human kind had faded.

He sat in quiet solitude as he peered out of the small window into the black void of space. All he could see was darkness and all he could hear was his own heart beating.

On earth I lay in my sleeping bag in the middle of Antarctica listening to deafening silence, only to be broken by my own heart beating.

To give up everything in life to follow a passion is a risky but inspiring move to make – and the rewards can be extraordinary.

Mark Wood – Explorer

Language… has created the word 'loneliness' to express the pain of being alone. And it has created the word 'solitude' to express the glory of being alone.

Paul Tillich

So It Begins...

Total isolation. It was 16.00 hours and the temperature a chilly -30°C as I stood in deep snow at my start point on the west coast of Antarctica. As I looked up into the clear blue sky I watched the Twin Otter plane circle around me twice as it seemed to point out the direction I needed to take before it flew back to Base Camp. This was my last human contact for 50 days. Silence followed its departure. A deafening silence, like a vacuum that filled my ears. After three years of preparing for this moment the stark reality kicked in as it became clear that this was it. I was finally all on my own.

I took my first look of what would be my home for the coming weeks, a brilliant white landscape trimmed by a cold blue horizon – the terrain flat with a glimpse of jagged ice formations gave it the look of a frozen lunar surface. I inhaled heavily and watched the heat from my breath as I exhaled in to the cold evening air. I felt alone – my heart beat quickly as I sensed both fear and excitement about where I was and what was about to happen – almost an instinct, a physical reaction to this most amazing of places.

Only 30 minutes earlier I had been in the middle of organised chaos at Base Camp, as the support team had scurried around to arrange all the logistical needs of the various explorers, climbers and researchers who were travelling through the site.

I was so relieved to finally be alone, without the pressure of having anyone judging me or analysing my every move. I stuck my ski poles in the snow and smiled, scanning the vast white horizon that lay before me. This is where my adventure truly began.

A thousand jumbled thoughts, helped to oust the appealing realisation that this was my first step of several million, my first breath of several billion.

Sir Ranulph Fiennes

In November 2011, I set off from Hercules Inlet on the west coast of Antarctica – my own mission statement outlined that I would attempt to become the first person in history to ski solo, unsupported and unaided, to both the Geographic South and the Geographic North Poles consecutively.

At the time only ten people in history had ever skied to the South Pole solo, unsupported and unaided (including great natural skiers such as Norwegians and Swedes... but no one from Coventry), and only two people had achieved this same approach to the North Pole, the Norwegian Børge Ousland (approaching from Russia) and Britain's Pen Haddow (from the Canadian coastline). I was setting my sights pretty high, hoping to carry out both expeditions, one immediately after the other.

Reaching the South Pole was only the first part of the journey. Within a few weeks of completing that arduous trek, my intention was to cross over broken sea ice and arrive at the North Pole within 65 days. If I'm honest, even though I had already completed over 15 major polar expeditions, nothing could have prepared me for what was about to happen.

My reason for setting such a record attempt was built not on ego, but on the need to create a significant platform from which to launch the education programmes I was developing with Skype to bring students around the world into my work space (see p.19 & 91).

Route

There are two recognised routes to the Geographic South Pole from the west coast of Antarctica, both logistically supported by ALE (Antarctic Logistics & Expeditions). The first is called the Nansen Route (named after Fridtjof Nansen, a great Norwegian explorer); the route I had chosen was 200 miles longer and departed from Hercules Inlet at 80 degrees south (700 miles or 612 nautical miles) from the South Pole.

The Hercules Inlet route is generally more recognised amongst fellow explorers. Of course, as exploration goes, you can set off from any point on the planet for your own personal journey – there isn't a rule book stating where you have to start. Both past and modern day explorers had enforced the point of setting off from a coastal area.

There are no specific measures or guidelines for explorers to follow as they set off to create their own journeys. When I was researching the Nansen Route as a possible alternative during the months of planning

---

Info Point: Nautical Miles
A nautical mile is based on the circumference of the earth, and is equal to one minute of latitude. It is slightly more than a statute (land measured) mile (1 nautical mile = 1.1508 statute miles). Nautical miles are used for charting and navigating.

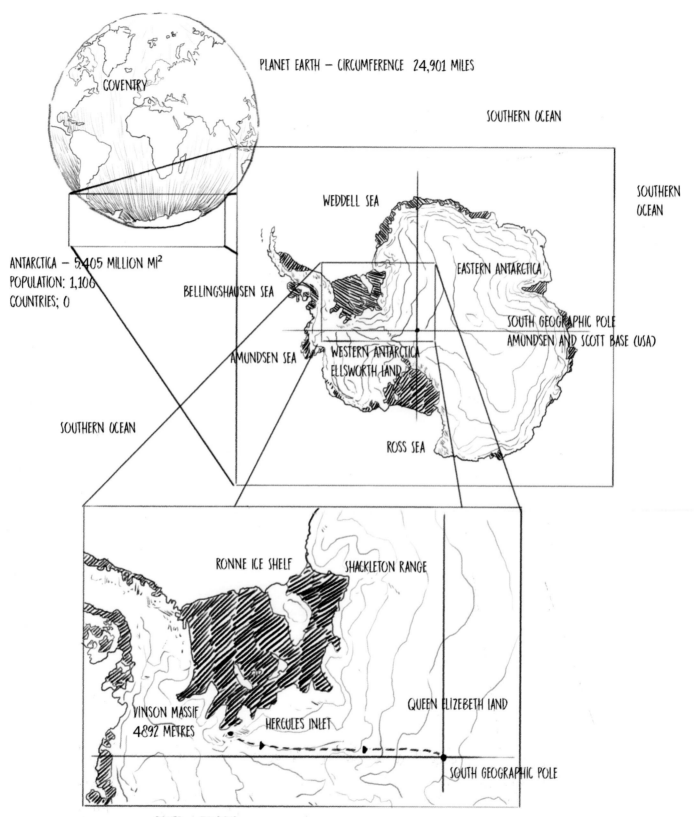

PLANET EARTH — CIRCUMFERENCE 24,901 MILES

COVENTRY

SOUTHERN OCEAN

SOUTHERN OCEAN

WEDDELL SEA

EASTERN ANTARCTICA

ANTARCTICA — 5.405 MILLION MI²
POPULATION: 1,106
COUNTRIES; 0

BELLINGSHAUSEN SEA

SOUTH GEOGRAPHIC POLE
AMUNDSEN AND SCOTT BASE (USA)

AMUNDSEN SEA

WESTERN ANTARCTICA
ELLSWORTH LAND

SOUTHERN OCEAN

ROSS SEA

RONNE ICE SHELF   SHACKLETON RANGE

QUEEN ELIZEBETH LAND

VINSON MASSIF
4892 METRES

HERCULES INLET

SOUTH GEOGRAPHIC POLE

ROUTE — 50 DAYS
612 NAUTICAL MILES / 704 STATUTE MILES

5

for this trip, I met up with a Canadian explorer called Richard Webber. Together with the great Russian explorer, Mikhail Malakhov, Richard completed an unsupported return expedition from the North Geographic Pole in 1995. This journey had never been done before and has not been repeated since. In total Richard has reached the Pole seven times, so his experience in the field is incredible.

I spoke to him about the two possible routes, and his advice had been that although every journey is personal, if I was to do this solo journey only once, then there could be no short cuts – it had to be the route from Hercules Inlet. I was trying to make history by reaching the two Poles, and what my peers would say meant a lot to me, so of course he was right.

Preparation

Every journey begins with the seed of an idea. That is the beauty of thinking differently, because it's easy to sit at home and dream of an adventure – anybody can do this. The skill, however, is making it happen. A major expedition, including the education and environmental awareness programmes, media support, marketing, filming and more can cost in excess of £200K to deliver, and as an unknown explorer trying to raise money and sponsorship, I need to be inspired so that I work hard to make that happen! Like many people, I can have that idea, that 'seed' in my head, but the skill is turning it into a reality.

Once I have that seed, I then take it to people that I trust, and with their help I outline the idea in more detail. I don't pretend to know it all, and to prevent getting tunnel-vision due to my own excitement, I need clear-headed people to analyse the plans and spot things that I am blind to. This is a continuing process leading up to the venture, up until the point that I am actually standing on rock or ice. I outline the timeline, costs, mission statement, and team, drawing all of my thoughts onto a white board so that I can look at it and then explain it further. In essence I empty my mind of ideas so that people I trust can then understand my plan – very much like setting up a new business.

Next we build a detailed proposal together, on the understanding that any companies I wish to approach are not stupid and will require a high level of planning and clarity. Above a certain level of funding, sponsoring companies are looking for a formal business proposal and will be evaluating how they can make a return on their investment. So it's important that I have my 'store' in order, with a strong website, brochures and branding so that the investors can have confidence in me and what I am planning to do.

In a sense, the easy part is the execution of the actual expedition, because I have built up all of that expertise through past expeditions. The hard part is inspiring the sponsors to invest. On the investor's side, it is a case of judging whether what I am doing fits in with what they want to do. If we can demonstrate to them that it does, then the budget itself isn't really a problem.

Two years is a good amount of time to prepare for a major expedition, and if I get it together in the first year, then that's great as it allows for time to train and gain media interest. However, the reality can be very different – the amount of set-backs and negativity can leave me questioning whether it was even a good idea in the first place. At this point, stepping back and re-assessing your approach to companies is a good idea. If you are passionate from the very beginning and believe that you will be out in the extremes, doing what you dreamed about, then it *will* happen.

Through my own experience, I've realised that no one can do it on their own, and you need the support of many other people – whilst at the same time understanding where your own skill set lies. My skills are in bringing teams together, developing them and pushing them forward. I help them to remain focussed and in doing this I bring in attributes of business life, such as good communication, leading from the back, and foreseeing possible problems – these are all part of logistical preparation and fund-raising before the trip even happens.

In the business world, when a company sets up a new venture, they go through all of this preparation and funding cycle. Usually they do not look to make a profit in the first two or three years of trading. I am trying to set up a new business every year, and so I am constantly working hard to do my best for the investors. You're only as good as the investors you have on board, and I try to deliver more than they expect, especially because I want them to remain on board for the next mission. Being an explorer is not just about walking across the ice and fighting off polar bears!

Info Point: 'Leading from the Back'
The expression 'leading from the back' in expedition or business terms is about understanding the individuals in you team and their own skill sets. A good leader will stand back and allow the team members to develop through the process without micro-managing them. This will allow them the freedom to utilise their own skills and ideas to push the project or expedition forward. It also allows them to feel that you are approachable for support when needed. On the leader's side, you can then have the clarity to assess the whole situation and guide the venture to success.

Mark Kelly and myself on training expeditions in the Arctic –
a perfect person to act as my South Pole logisitcs and liason.

The first actual physical step of my adventure to the South Pole began on a flight from London to Punta Arenas, which is a stopover on the way through to Antarctica. Located at the southern tip of Chile, both Shackleton and Scott had used Punta Arenas on their journeys to the South Pole. The city is well known for its red-painted metal roofs and has a bizarre mixture of out-dated British colonial architecture with heavy Spanish influences.

To accompany me on my preparation for the journey, I took along a good friend and fellow adventurer, Mark Kelly. Mark had been on expeditions with me for ten years and not only had he walked and skied alongside me, but he had used his own experience to set up the links to schools around the world from the extremes we were working in. A lot of credit has been directed at me for what we have achieved, but Mark stands out as the real work force that made the expeditions accessible to everybody.

During our week together in Punta Arenas, Mark and I experienced some teething problems with the logistics company I was using. We felt as if they had decided that I did not quite fit the bill of the lean, athletic explorer they had in mind. My extra weight was in fact planned so that when I reached the South Pole, I would then have a good body mass and strength to complete the North Pole leg. Even in my condition I was still running four to six miles a day and maintaining a good overall fitness! All of my polar experience had been in the American, Canadian and Norwegian High Arctic, so this was my first time heading south. I was unknown to them and it seemed that I posed a certain risk to their company reputation if they allowed me to go ahead on my own.

Put under the microscope and feeling patronised, Mark Kelly played the peacemaker. The logistics company were worried about me going solo and lacked faith in what I could achieve – in their eyes there was too much risk involved. I allowed them to do whatever they had to in order to ease their minds, as ultimately they were only looking after my interests, and on reflection I understood their concerns and respected them for it. My stay in Punta Arenas was an unnecessary stressful time, and when the logistics company finally told me that the plane was leaving, I was relieved but also a bundle of nerves inside.

Two nights before my departure at 2 o'clock in the morning Mark woke me up and told me that he had to go to the airport and head back to the UK – his flight was due and so my only companion was heading home. We shook hands (as the British do) and then I gave him a hug – saying goodbye for me was a pretty sad moment, and all of a sudden I felt alone.

The flight to Union Glacier Base was on an Ilyushin aircraft, a four-engine jet built by the Russians for the very worst of Siberian winters. The trip takes four to five hours, and the plane was jam-packed full of

equipment and people, including researchers, scientists, film crews, explorers, and the occasional mountain climber bound for Mount Vinson. On the Ilyushin, without windows, surrounded by our equipment, we felt like we were in a military craft.

The plane landed at 4.00 am on a hard blue ice runway at Union Glacier Base Camp where the temperature was warmer than I had expected at -10°C with a very light wind – ideal for pitching tents and getting organised. Looking around there was the most stunning scenery of snowy mountains surrounding the camp, and the main mess tent had good food, hot showers, washing and laundry services. It was like a home-from-home to a degree as I settled in and pitched my tent. However, by the following day I was itching to get moving.

A year previously I trained from the most northern settlements in the world in the town of Longyearbyen, situated on the Svalbard Islands (halfway between the tip of Norway and the North Pole itself). Whilst there, a great American explorer, Doug Stoup, advised me that when you arrive at Union Glacier, be ready to go. The more time you spend there, the more you will be nervous. Head out and immerse yourself in the journey. The initial fear you have of the next step is key, and it is crucial to make that step!

Being flown in a Twin Otter plane to the start point of the expedition, my final moments with other human beings

As the Twin Otter plane took off I had a bird's-eye view of Union Glacier, watching people waving goodbye as 'that British guy on his own' (who looked pretty scared) headed out. The 30-minute flight allowed me to watch the ice below and scan the white void that I was about to be dropped into. Inside the plane all seemed busy, but in the sky the aircraft appeared so insignificant against the vast openness of the Antarctic continent.

Before take-off, I was busy packing my tent away when I felt a tap on my shoulder – I looked round at a Norwegian girl who had been helping with our flight plans and behind her were five other people, just looking straight at me. She said, "We are ready for you now Mark." It's strange to say, but my fear concerning what was about to happen was so strong that it made me feel like a condemned man accompanied by his smiling guards, waiting to be led to his execution – a dead man walking!

As I froze on the spot in front of her she asked, "Are you ok?" "I feel pretty scared," I replied quietly. She then said something that I dismissed straight away, and it was only on the last day of the expedition as I approached the South Pole that I then understood what she meant. "Mark, you're living your dream…!"

At the start point of Hercules Inlet we circled two or three times, checking the ice for a safe place to land. The landing gear opened and the plane bumped along the ice. Keeping the engine running, we unloaded the equipment as the rest of the crew walked the runway to ensure that it was safe to fly off again.

Over the last 50 years the west coast's annual mean temperature has risen by three degrees, making it one of most rapidly warming parts of the planet. My expedition was partly about providing a first-hand account

The ALE team take a last photograph of me from the drop-off plane.
The single speck of me can be seen on the middle left hand-side of the picture.

Saying goodbye as I head into the Antarctic void towards the Pole

of what changes were happening in the area, as I hoped to not only increase awareness of the various projects that my team and I had set up before departing, but also to open a window for people to see for themselves the change that our planet is experiencing. Like many people, I hear about the effects of climate change. However, until you have seen it for yourself and come face-to-face with the damage that has already taken place, it can be difficult to fully appreciate the reality.

One of the key environmental issues is to try to humanise the consequences of climate change for people who feel that they are detached from the situation. My journey, though not scientific, focused on communicating honestly what I could see and how I felt. In this way people could relate to who I was as an ordinary person, which would then allow me to highlight how they are actually a part of the problem – we are all connected and involved in the changing climate of our planet.

I was the only one to be dropped off at that time, and as I climbed from the plane I concentrated on how not to mess this up, acutely aware of all these eyes on me. My body was feeling heavy and uncoordinated – I probably looked incompetent in front of these very fit and seasoned Antarctic personnel. I thanked them all as they had been so supportive, and now as I look back on that moment I know they weren't judging me – they simply wanted the best for me. I said my final 'goodbyes' to people who were complete strangers, although thanks to the unique circumstances, I actually felt extremely close to them because they would be my last human contact for a very long time.

During the flight I had handed a memory card for a camera and an envelope with Mark Kelly's home address written on it to one of the crew on the plane. I wanted them to take photos of me leaving and then send them on to Mark to use on our social media and expedition updates (see later in 'Halfway' chapter).

I strapped on my harness and, aware that I was being watched, began to move forward. The sledge felt too heavy and my heart began to race as my body experienced the shock of exercise. I just wanted the others to leave so that I could scream. I felt like they were thinking, "Who does this guy think he is? We will see him back within a week!"

When I set off on an expedition, I don't plan to cover a set amount of miles each day – the journey is too unpredictable that early on. Placing my body and equipment under too much strain and pressure from the start can have significant implications for the whole expedition, so I did not want to set myself up for failure. I had planned to kick each day off with a fairly easy routine of targets, getting up at 8.00 am and finishing at 6.00 pm during the first few weeks. On nearing the Pole I would then adjust my schedule to make sure that I made my destination by day 50. This plan meant that I switched from working off a set time schedule in the first part of the expedition, to then assessing the mileage I had left in the latter part. During this second stage I would divide up the total mileage up so that I had a set amount of miles to complete each day before I set up my nightly camp. The key was to make things as easy as possible for myself and release any unnecessary pressure.

Of course, on day one I was not aware that due to unknown reasons I had been dropped 30 nautical miles back from where I had expected to be dropped. This was a considerable amount of mileage – if you add to this that I had packed my food and cooker fuel for 50 days' walking, with an additional emergency pack if things went completely wrong, 30 miles could add a possible two or three days to the journey and would have been psychologically damaging at the start. Realisation of this fact only became apparent on the evening of day one when I re-checked my positioning.

I could not have started out in better weather – the skies were clear, there was no wind, and I had perfect visibility. I travelled for three hours before stopping to pitch my tent and call in to Base Camp to notify them that I was safe and well. During these nightly calls (which would continue through the expedition), the very least I would give was my position, how I was and my direction of travel (south). This was in case of an emergency pickup when I had not made my scheduled call and needed to be located by the rescue team. They could then judge from my last reported location that I would be in a 10 to 15 nautical mile radius – it limits their search zone. Anyway, after this first haul I had covered just 3.4 nautical miles – but at least I was on my way.

My back was cramping from dragging a fully laden 120 kg 'pulk' (Finnish for pulkka or sledge) together with a 15 kg rucksack, but I was feeling confident that it wouldn't take too long for me to toughen up. I kept part of the weight (mainly the fuel) on my back to ease the drag of the pulk.

However, as I started out, I have to admit that I felt really out of condition. My expedition was to take place on both sides of the planet, but sitting over my core fitness and muscle was a layer of essential fat which would burn off within a few weeks. So progress would be slow to begin with!

At the end of the first day I set up my tent (my home), a Hilleberg tunnel-tent designed so that strong winds would pass around, in much the same way as a sports car is designed. These are perfect for polar work when the wind direction can be predictable, although not so good in mountains where the direction is unpredictable. It was snug and there was bright sunshine outside as I settled down for my first night. At 3.00 am a snowstorm broke out and the wind whipped severely across the tent. It felt like Antarctica had really come alive around me, letting me know that it was in charge.

Opposite: Our unexpected guest in the most remote community in the Canadian Arctic – Fritz (far right) was a humble legend
Below: The Inuit hamlet of Gris Fiord camouflaged by coastal rocks and sea ice

Theory of Training

No training can truly prepare the mind and body for journeys of this kind. A unique viewpoint about physical preparation was given by Yorkshireman Sir Wally Herbert, one of the greatest polar explorers of the last century, a man who led the Trans-Arctic Expedition in 1969 which went down in polar history as the first team ever to cross the North Geographic Pole (an honour recognised by The Royal Geographic Society), 60 years after Robert Peary's disputed attempt. Sir Herbert once said that he would rather spend the first five to ten days of an expedition going through enormous hardship than spending a year training for it. The Trans-Arctic journey was unfortunately not great news at the time, because in the same year three men landed on the Moon, out-trumping Sir Herbert's remarkable achievement.

A few years before the North and South Pole expeditions, both Mark Kelly and myself were running an Arctic schools programme in Gris Fiord, the highest Inuit settlement in the Canadian High Arctic. One afternoon we sat in the kitchen drinking coffee as a tall burly-looking chap walked in, who turned out to be Fritz Koerner, the fourth member of The Trans-Arctic Expedition. To meet him and chat about the expedition in such a unique area was such a privilege. We found out that just a few months later Fritz had unfortunately died – another unsung hero that had truly lived his life.

As Sir Wally Herbert had highlighted, the first week of any expedition is the toughest as the body adjusts to the new routine and grows all the stronger for it. When delivering talks to schools, I tell the students that the first part of anything they do can be tough – such as moving to a new school or new class, or eventually when they finish education and take their first steps into the outside world. My advice is take your time and do not be afraid to make mistakes – embrace fear, as it's a way of sharpening you up for what is about to happen. Persist and, most importantly, enjoy.

What Is an Explorer?

What it means to be an 'explorer' in the twenty-first century is quite different to what it used to mean. In a sense, anyone can be an adventurer today – if you have the experience, time and the money, you can take a trip to the Poles, you can ascend Everest, you can trek across deserts, jungles and oceans. Then you can return home and carry on working. This is the sensible option, especially as you are possibly getting paid at the same time!

However, I do this full time. I set my stall out as 'Mark Wood – Explorer', and as such, I need to have good reasons for doing so. Traditional exploration, going back into the eighteenth, nineteenth and twentieth centuries, was about 'discovery'. Of course, my expeditions can still be about discovery – discovering the effects of global warming, discovering the best way to do a particular challenge… and of course there is always *self*-discovery.

Self-discovery is perhaps as important as geographical discovery. Without any grandeur or self-promotion, the ability to discover truths about yourself in the midst of an expedition is quite unparalleled.

With self-discovery sits *re*-discovery. I very much believe that I have been walking in the footsteps of giants, the likes of the Norwegian Roald Amundsen and the British explorer Captain Robert Falcon-Scott, heading off on journeys with a real sense of history. These pioneers should not be forgotten, and modern day explorations can bring home the fantastic achievements that happened in a world before computer chips, GPS and technical fabrics.

However, perhaps most important to my sense of being an explorer is education. I am not a teacher – I didn't go to university, and I don't set myself up in parallel or in competition with the very gifted teachers that we have. Nevertheless, what inspires me day in and day out is a desire to share what I have learnt – to show the world how it really is. When I give a talk at a school, or I chat to children via Skype around the world and see them fired up, this is when I feel comfortable calling myself an explorer.

No matter where I am around the world on expedition there are three main areas I concentrate on to inspire students. *Firstly*, how modern day explorers operate, and why there is still a need for them. *Secondly*, trying to bring the extremes of the planet into the classroom – hoping that the children can feel and see what I am seeing, focusing on cultural differences and the changes of climate, and helping them to see the planet from a different point of view. And *thirdly*, giving the students a sense of aspiration. Here am I, a normal person born in Coventry in the UK, far removed from mountains, sea or ice, yet I am involved in these extraordinary expeditions. I'm like this because I think differently about life. The children I see in the classroom may not end up being explorers, but they have a whole world of opportunity. We live in an incredible era of choice that gives children so many chances – they can become who they want to be.

This desire or passion is highlighted in a wonderful quote from the late great pioneer of technology, Steve Jobs. On May 30th 2007 at a D5 Conference, 'All Things Digital' he said,

People say you have a lot of passion for what you're doing and it's totally true... it's so hard, that if you don't, any rational person would give up.

I want students to be 'explorers' in that sense, to conquer their own 'Everest'. Don't focus on fame, getting rich quickly or having instant success. Life isn't like that. If you have a passion for what you are doing, you can cope with any obstacle, and success and enjoyment will follow. Inspire yourselves to inspire others.

When I returned from the South Pole expedition, I received an email from a man in Central America. I had no idea who he was but he had heard about the solo attempt on Facebook. He and his family followed me, day-by-day, listening to the daily updates and charting my progress before his children went off to school. What he wanted to know was, now that I had finished the expedition, what should he show his children next?

This was wonderful. Small things like this really keep me focused on the fact that maybe I am doing things right, and this father's comments are a true reason for me to continue to explore.

Connecting students 3,500 metres high in the Nepalese mountains with a school in Japan

It's easy to have 'famous' heroes in life, but those who inspire me most are as much the 'unsung heroes' as the well-known people of history books. *An Unsung Hero* is the life story of Irishman Tom Crean, born in 1877, and who ran away to sea at the age of 15 to eventually spend more time in the Antarctic than either Scott or Shackleton. He was the workhorse behind these great men, but he didn't seek fame – his personal goal was to set up a pub in his hometown of Annascaul in Ireland. It still stands today, and is called 'The South Pole Inn'. I visited the pub on my return from the South Pole and after toasting him over a pint of Guinness, I took a drive just a few short miles in the rain to his resting place. As I walked through the graveyard that was coated in green moss, I made my way to the far corner, next to the sound of a running stream. I stood in silence in front of his tomb. The sound of the wind and rain was fitting for the journeys that this man had taken in his life – I felt a small connection in knowing the areas he had worked in. I felt a calmness, and the rain and wind seemed to stop for a brief while as I walked back to my car. He was the shadow and the strength on those historic pioneering expeditions. Now *he* is a hero to me.

A hero is an everyday person who thinks of others with small and kind acts of faith and kindness. I'm inspired as much by that person, as I am by an Olympian bringing back a medal for his or her own nation. I tell students that everything that will happen in their lives will come from within. To be a good decent human being is the springboard to a full life.

I'm certainly not in the exploring game for the fame or the money. I used to live in a house that I was renovating which had no furniture, running water or kitchen – instead I had four sledges, a few large bags of expedition gear and a camping cooker. I didn't think about essential items at the time because I was driven by my next project. However, there is a fine line between being inspired by your work and neglecting your home life and family. Part of success is getting the balance in life right.

An unsung hero, Tom Crean

Getting into My Stride (Day Two/Three)

Out on my own on ice, I was excited with what lay ahead of me, and the responsibility of setting my own routine for the next few weeks. The key to a long-range expedition is to get into a routine as soon as possible. I planned to do an hour of skiing, followed by a five-minute break. The reality was hard – I was skiing uphill from sea level with a heavy pulk, and there were strong katabatic winds coming across glaciers which were blowing straight off the South Pole plateau and heading towards me. Every day I experienced a head-wind to the point that I just accepted it, as I had no other choice. The best female polar explorer in the world, Matty McNair, who lives in the Canadian High Arctic in Iqaluit on Baffin Island, said to me, "Heading to the South Pole is just a long hard slog." Ahead of me the land was full of crevasses, so to avoid this I had to 'dog-leg' off course to an arbitrary point before I could turn again and head south. This in itself presented a psychological wall, fighting the strong temptation to just head straight south, but as I was alone the safer, though longer, option, was the one I was on. Trying to struggle out from a crevasse on my own with a fully loaded pulk was not really wise.

By the evening of the second day I had covered good ground, making 7.5 nautical miles. However, my left knee was already hurting as it had been damaged a few months previously during an earthquake scare on a trip to

---

Info Point: 'Katabatic Wind'
Katabatic wind (from the Greek katabaino – to go down) is the generic term for downslope winds flowing from high elevations of mountains, plateaus, and hills down their slopes to the valleys or plains below.

the Himalayas. As I was sitting in a lodge 3,800 metres up in the mountains, the building waved and moved like a fairground fun house. I ran down the corridors with the Sherpas as the lights flickered on and off. The deafening sound of the lodge shifting was terrifying. As we jumped out of the main doors, I realised my client was still in the basement, so I ran back in and dragged him out a few minutes later, just as the quake began to relax. During those adrenaline-fuelled minutes my knee had been damaged so severely that we had to abort the climb, and this was only a few months before the South Pole attempt. Back in the UK my friend and occupational therapist Richard Watson (from the company *Apache Brave*) worked on me constantly to rapidly prepare me for Antarctica. I owe him a lot, but the terrain was trying to undo all of his good work.

The same day as my knee injury flared up I had picked up a deep cough, and in addition the food wasn't agreeing with me so I was also feeling sick. I had reduced the food intake for the beginning of the trip, as my body system was not ready for full expedition high calorific food, but even reduced rations had an adverse effect on me.

At least I was dry, warm and hydrated, and mercies such as these allowed me to feel happy in my own little world. As would become my daily routine, I radioed in to Base Camp to confirm my coordinates in a very brief call, when I would listen to one of the very few voices I heard during the whole trip.

The next day brought disaster – not a bad injury, not getting lost, not falling through ice… but losing my iPod! It was as simple as that, but had the potential to damage the success of the expedition. I'm not sure exactly how it happened, but I remember frantically going through all my equipment – it was just gone. And of course the colour of my iPod… white! Mark Kelly had previously loaded all my music, radio podcasts and photos onto the iPod. I was extremely disappointed at the time and saw the loss of this little device as a huge obstacle. When I go 'outside', whether it's in the mountains in Wales and Scotland, overseas, or even just walking my dogs, I don't normally listen to music – not even on long car journeys. However, when faced with just under 600 nautical miles of nothing, you need the occasional mental stimulation!

360° of nothing

I had no idea how I was going to occupy my mind through those endless, freezing hours that I would spend dragging a dead weight through ice. The last song I listened to before I lost the iPod was 'Wait in Vain' by Bob Marley, a song that stayed in my head throughout my days on the ice.

The physiological strain of losing sound got to me on the fifth day. As I sat in my tent I looked at the slow progress I was making, the fact that I was also not heading south due to navigating around the crevasse fields, and other issues such as feeling heavy, weak, and sick. If losing my iPod wasn't bad enough, I had also snapped my ski bindings. In short, I was looking for an excuse to give up.

I spent 36 hours in my tent contemplating giving up – the task I had set for myself seemed impossible. I called up Mark Kelly and blurted out half-a-dozen excuses, explaining that I had little option but to call Base Camp and get picked up – to abort the expedition. I wanted him to tell me that I had done everything I could and that I should pack up and come home.

Mark was actually at work in London when I called. He responded perfectly by telling me about the amount of interest I was receiving in the UK, and how the Global Schools Programme was following my route. He continued for several minutes of precious battery time, bringing me back to reality, and reminding me that it was still my first week and that I had not given the expedition a real chance. Mark reminded me how people had invested time and effort in helping get me there, and that I couldn't let them down with shoddy excuses. I bleated that my binding was broken – again, I reasoned that I had no choice but to call in the rescue planes.

Everything Mark said was all very positive and he refused to agree with an ounce of the nonsense I was throwing at him. He told me to take a second look at my bindings, and with a clearer head I simply moved them back half an inch to a new section of the ski and screwed them back in – it was in fact so simple that I wanted to slap myself for not thinking of it. I hadn't really been looking for solutions – only excuses.

I also phoned my dad in desperation that someone would tell me to come home, but to my surprise Dad almost shouted down the phone and told me to keep going. I think he was shouting because Antarctica was a long way away! I was really left with only one choice.

Mark managed to talk me through each issue and in the end I had no excuses. I put one ski in front of the other and continued on. The easy option would have been to call the plane in and then to make the equipment failure a little more exaggerated. Mark's central message to me was the number of students worldwide who were following my journey and how I shouldn't really let them down – cheers Mark!

Continuing that same day after counting 3,000 ski steps I stopped in my tracks and said out loud, "This is a nightmare – all I am doing is counting steps." So I closed my eyes with 360 degrees of nothing around me and thought about where I would liked to have been at that moment in time. I saw myself with my dogs walking through a childhood haunt in the pine forests near Wells-next-the-Sea in Norfolk, England. I began skiing, smelling the pine and sensing the fresh breeze of the ocean as it drifted over me. I continued this for several hours and when I came out of it I was back in Antarctica having covered over 5.7 nautical miles of ice.

At various times during my journey I drifted off into six different dreamscapes, including re-decorating my house, guiding teams in the Himalayas or delivering talks to schools. I believe this was a major contribution to my success in reaching the Pole.

When I returned from the expedition I worked with psychologist Dr Harbinder Sandu on the impact of working alone in the extremes. We based the studies on the daily updates that I had recorded each evening on the ice into a dictaphone. Dr Harbinder then spent hours interviewing me and wrote a proposal to turn the findings into an academic paper. Along with Peter Suedfeld, Lisa Shiozaki and Ben Archdekin from Columbia University, a paper was eventually published in the *Polar Journal*.*

The conclusion to the article is interesting for two reasons: firstly, the authors concluded that I never mentioned craving companionship during the journey – I seemed to be comfortable being alone. And secondly, that it is difficult to make general conclusions on their study alone, as they would need more people to go out on solo expeditions for this period of time and similarly be open to studies – which is unlikely. As they conclude:

> As with any idiographic study, the generalisability of the results reported here is an open question. Explorers are different from a representative sample of the human population, and solo explorers are arguably different from most explorers. To what extent Wood is similar to others of his ilk cannot be ascertained unless and until other people undertaking similar adventures provide diaries that undergo similar analyses. This early quantitative study is one step along the way to a more general portrait.

---

* Peter Suedfeld, Lisa Shiozaki, Ben Archdekin, Harbinder Sandhu & Mark Wood (2017): 'The Polar Exploration Diary of Mark Wood: A Thematic Content Analysis', The Polar Journal
To access this journal online go to http://dx.doi.org/10.1080/2154896X.2017.1333327.

What Is Alone?

There are degrees of isolation in all manner of situations – people being captured, astronauts spinning around the earth in small capsules, or people who feel alone in the midst of a city full of thousands of people. There is a vast difference between feeling alone and being isolated. On the South Pole trip I wasn't lonely, but I was as isolated as I could be from the rest of the planet. The previously mentioned academic paper observed the following about me:

> He does not seem to crave human companionship; his motivation is focused on achieving his goal.

I had spent 30 days training for this solo expedition by trying to be alone in Svalbard, Norway. Whilst there I would often come across other tracks, and I could hear the faint rumble of skidoos. The temptation to head back into the town for a coffee was overwhelming, and it was only human nature to do that. So I wasn't really being entirely honest with the experience of being on my own. The difference with this trip was that when I was dropped in, I had no real option of dropping out. Sometimes in 'normal life' we are thrown into situations that we feel are virtually impossible to get out of – experience and the ability to step back and think clearly are essential to pushing through these testing moments.

As I stood *truly alone* for the first time, I distinctly remember squeezing my eyes shut for a few moments, as waves of terror engulfed my mind. It took several deep breaths for me to centre myself and gain control over the fear that had built up. I forced myself to focus on what, at that particular moment, was good. I was alone – I had no one to watch me make the mistakes I would no doubt make, and no team to worry about. It was just me – and that's just how I wanted it. This expedition had taken years of planning, all culminating into this single moment where I was to begin my solo journey on ice.

A snow bath in the middle of solo training

The World's Most Remote Places

If you stand on a pier and feel the strength of the ocean against you, then that's a real powerful thing; if you stand in the Arctic and feel the cold, the intensity, the remoteness, that too is remarkable. The force of Mother Nature in the extremes makes you feel how insignificant you actually are.

The world we live in is so crowded with information, and a normal person's whole day can be crammed full of stimulus. From the moment you wake you gather information through your senses concerning colours, sounds and smells. Imagine taking all of that away – standing in a white void alone where even your sense of depth is blurred as your mind finds it difficult to judge distances across a white landscape. When you finally tune into where you are your senses are heightened, and your mind is as clear as a blank canvass – it's only when you get back to civilisation that you realise how powerful those experiences are.

The Polar regions in their purity can be quiet and relaxing… but within an instant they can turn aggressive and dangerous. Having completed a few Polar expeditions over the years, I completely understand that I am totally insignificant in comparison to that landscape, and so with this I have developed a tremendous respect for the polar regions.

My home in the coldest of places – you can see the pure joy on my face!

From Bad to Worse

At the start of the trek, it was tough to get going every day – my knee had swelled under the initial strain and I was in pain for a good part of each morning. I had not expected it to play up so early on and I wondered how I was going to manage nearly 50 days of this. My sickness was improving because I was craving food and my body was adjusting to the drastic increase in calories.

On day three I stupidly miscalculated my bearing, climbed up a hill dragging my pulk behind me, and added two hours to my journey (not to mention using all that extra energy). On the other side of the hill, it seemed like it was only a short slope down a 20-metre drop, so I let my pulk slide all the way down. Due to the inability to perceive distance accurately in a white landscape, I watched in horror as the pulk kept sliding down until it was the size of a pinhead. Thankfully it was undamaged, but a mistake like that could have cost me the expedition.

To further my problems, my ski bindings snapped again, but this time it was the toe bar that had come apart. This is where the boot attaches and pivots to the ski, and it's a really crucial area. If you're covering hundreds of miles on ice, skis will allow you to use less energy and cover more ground. Less energy means less food intake, and so in principle a lighter pulk. Just wearing boots would have an opposite effect. I think the bindings snapped because I didn't have Norwegian blood running through me and as a Brit I tended to ski like an elephant. There is a photograph of me taken using a self-timer where I am kneeling, but as I stood up from the shot I felt the bar 'ping' – it might have been this moment of kneeling at a different angle that finally broke it (see picture on page 46).

In total the bindings and toe bar must have snapped over 15 times during the whole journey. The style of boot / binding allowed me to back-country ski, which is all about pushing the ski forward from your toe as your heal lifts off the ski itself. (This is as good a description as you will get from an Englishman – for more technical advice speak to a Norwegian or a Swede!)

Rather than throw in the towel, hearing Mr Kelly's voice in my head I began to work through each situation carefully. At times I might set up my tent at midday to give me shelter and then make a cup of tea so that I could relax from my anxiety before coming up with solutions about how to fix these issues – all with no support team or local hardware shop!

If my time in the Fire and Rescue Service at Windsor Fire Station taught me anything, it was how to be resourceful. I used the guy lines of my tent, straps off my pulk, elastic cords from my clothing and screws from any bit of equipment that had them to make sure my boot remained on the ski. At one point I burnt a hole in the toe of the boot to get a better purge for binding them together. It was an ongoing job, but it worked.

With little specialist equipment, I cut, burnt and bound my skis and boots throughout the journey....

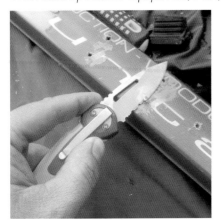
The knife of many uses

Boot laces to secure bindings

Tent guy lines tighten the bond

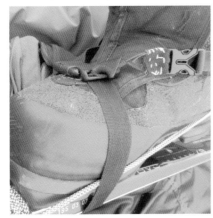
Strap from my sledge allows the boot to lever on the ski

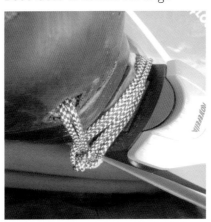
Burning a small hole in the toe added a stronger link

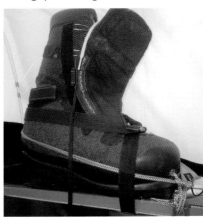
Side-ways movement prevented me using more tent guy lines

Each day began to roll into another. After the first week my routine was simple but effective – just as it should be. With every third day there was generally a white-out, and sometimes I could see it coming as a wall of mist heading straight for me. I would squint through my goggles thinking that there was a long cliff in front of me, approaching at speed, and then within seconds I was surrounded by white!

It's difficult to explain exactly what being in a white-out is like. In the film *The Matrix*, there is a scene where the two main characters, Morpheus and Neo, enter a virtual room where they 'upload' themselves with weapons. The room is like a blank canvass. This is the closest example I can give. There are no distinguishing features, and the horizon, the ground and the sky, all merge into one. It's just a white space with nothing to see except the colour white. I didn't know how to cope as I skied slowly forward like a blind man.

Navigation at this point is difficult but not impossible. Working off a GPS bearing to give me direction of travel, I would usually revert to my compass to maintain my direction. A compass is good until you get closer to the Pole because the lines of latitude become closer together. This causes the magnetic variation to increase – it could go up to 30%, compared to just 3% in the UK. When there are no reference points to make the compass useful, then wind or ice can be used to navigate.

For most days the single blue line was my vision

White-outs left me with few navigation options

A compass works as long as there is a reference point

Info Point: 'White-out'
White-out has been defined as: "A condition of diffuse light when no shadows are cast, due to a continuous white cloud layer appearing to merge with the white snow surface. No surface irregularities of the snow are visible, but a dark object may be clearly seen. There is no visible horizon." – The Crossing of Antarctica by Sir Vivian Fuchs and Sir Edmund Hillary (London: Cassell, 1958), 296

Hauling my heavy pulk behind me

My good friend Jon Geldart, who skied to the Geomagnetic Pole with me back in the day, and his wife Clare, had given me a small yellow ribbon before I left as a symbol to come home safely. I had tied the ribbon to my ski pole and as the wind blew it gave me an aid to stay on my bearing.

The ice formation below my skis consisted of small long grooves, much the same as you would find on a sandy beach. This formation on ice is called sastrugi, and when you lay straight skis across sastrugi you can calculate your direction of travel – if the ice below you changes angle or the ribbon blows towards you, then you know that you are heading in the wrong direction.

Sitting in your arm chair reading this, it might seem technical to navigate like this, but when you're living the journey day-to-day, it's quite simple and becomes almost second nature.

Jon and Clare Geldart's yellow ribbon allowed me to navigate in white-outs using only the wind

Info Point: 'Sastrugi'
Sastrugi, or zastrugi, are sharp irregular grooves or ridges formed on a snow surface by wind erosion, saltation of snow particles, and deposition, and found in polar and open sites such as frozen lakes in cold temperate regions. The ridges are usually parallel to the prevailing winds – they are steep on the windward side and sloping to the leeward side. Smaller irregularities of this type are known as ripples (small, 10 mm high) or wind ridges.

Dealing with Fear

The feeling of fear will keep you alive – it will awaken your senses. The closer I got to departing for the South Pole, the more petrified I became. But fear is something we all experience, in a wide range of circumstances, and something that we learn to cope with.

When I was a firefighter we were trained to deal with situations without emotion. When you approach an incident such as a multiple car pile up on a motorway, you are taught to appraise the situation professionally, and deal with the incident methodically. The main priorities being first your own safety and that of your crew, and then after this comes the safety of the casualties involved. You are constantly assessing the levels of danger, and through experience and training the extraction of emotion allows you to think about the incident practically. Inner fear however is different – it prevents you from making rash decisions.

The job used to be called the 'Fire Brigade', but with less fires and more car accidents and other incidents, it changed to the 'Fire and Rescue Service', covering (in my opinion) many grey areas. Basically we had to work as a team to be able to cope with any situation. One such event was totally unexpected.

RBFR, Windsor Fire Station
I'm on the far right

33

During rush hour on the M4 heading into London we attended a car fire in the pouring rain. The police were in attendance and asked our watch to move all of our equipment to the hard shoulder. A car was being chased by the police and they were throwing metal stingers down to stop the vehicle by bursting the tyres. We watched from a distance as two officers struggled to get the two suspects out of the immobilised car.

The car windows had been smashed and one of the officers had cuts all over his arm. All four lanes on either side of the motorway had come to a standstill in the pouring rain, and all eyes were on the incident.

We felt the need to support the police so we blocked the car with the fire engine to prevent a get-away attempt. I stood behind the police and a medic attending the officer's arms when suddenly the medic looked at me and shouted, "He's got a gun!" From the front driver's side all three men dispersed together, leaving me exposed to the suspects and a possible gun.

Afterwards the crew said that they had been shouting at me to get away, but I took my helmet off and started to hit the two guys with it, knocking one of them unconscious. The adrenaline was working overtime. Both suspects were eventually arrested, having escaped from prison a few weeks earlier. A short while later the gun was found on the floor of the car.

There are two forms of decision-making – the first is where you need to react quickly, based on training and experience. The second is when you have time to step back, assess and even bring in other like-minded people to run through options. In both situations you need to be able to justify your actions.

I sometimes hear people giving their opinion on leadership decisions made on expeditions, all safely from the comfort of their own armchairs. However, in extreme situations you have to make decisions based on many factors that are happening in that singular moment.

In the film *Sully* based on a true story, Captain Chesley Sullenberger ('Sully', played by Tom Hanks) had just a few seconds to assess the damage to the commercial plane he was in command of as its engines failed with 155 souls on board. As they flew over Manhattan he checked the amount of fuel compared to distance to the nearest runways. All the time his mind must have been focused on the passengers and crew. He decided to land the plane in the Hudson River, an unprecedented manoeuvre that resulted in no lives lost.

In the official hearing shortly after the event, Sully was criticised for his actions as they went against the manual guidelines. He justified his decision based on years of flying experience, but most importantly on the fact that he had a complete understanding of the moment.

Never be frightened to make a decision – the worst thing you can do is do nothing.

Info Point: 'Watch'
A designated shift of firefighters at a station. In most UK fire services the watches are blue, red, white and green.

Gris Fiord – Resolute Bay

When I eventually left the Fire and Rescue Service and tried to set up on my own to run polar and mountain expeditions, my main concern at this early stage of exploration was how I could transpose my expedition experience back into classrooms worldwide.

The only technology at the time for me to use was a satellite phone. During an expedition with another adventurer friend, Ryan Scarratt, we led the first team to link the two highest Inuit settlements in the Canadian High Arctic. This was along a recognised trading route for Inuit guides and polar bear hunters that either used dog teams or skidoos to make their way through. Nobody outside of the Inuit community had ever attempted the 300-mile trek man-hauling pulks… and why should they?!

Philip de-Berger, Ryan Scarratt and Ian Hibberd crossing the North-West Passage with me to Gris Fiord

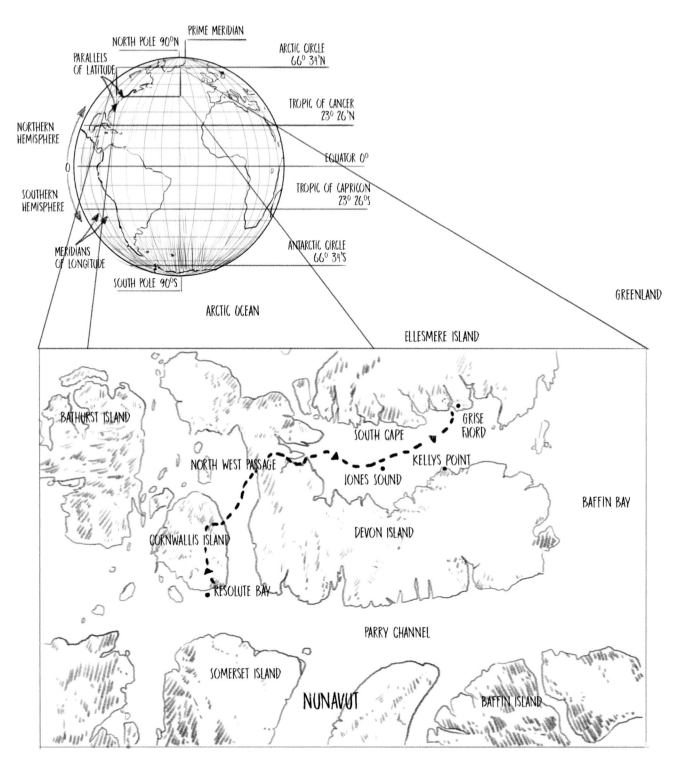

NORTH POLE 90°N

PRIME MERIDIAN

PARALLELS
OF LATITUDE

ARCTIC CIRCLE
66° 34'N

TROPIC OF CANCER
23° 26'N

NORTHERN
HEMISPHERE

EQUATOR 0°

TROPIC OF CAPRICON
23° 26'S

SOUTHERN
HEMISPHERE

MERIDIANS
OF LONGITUDE

ANTARCTIC CIRCLE
66° 34'S

SOUTH POLE 90°S

ARCTIC OCEAN

GREENLAND

ELLESMERE ISLAND

BATHURST ISLAND

SOUTH CAPE

GRISE
FIORD

NORTH WEST PASSAGE

KELLYS POINT

JONES SOUND

BAFFIN BAY

CORNWALLIS ISLAND

DEVON ISLAND

RESOLUTE BAY

PARRY CHANNEL

SOMERSET ISLAND

NUNAVUT

BAFFIN ISLAND

RESOLUTE BAY — 74.6973° N, 94.8297° W
GRISE FIORD — 76.4190° N, 82.9016° W
EXPEDITION ROUTE DISTANCE TO GRISE FIORD — 300 NAUTICAL MILES
DURATION — 28 DAYS

The start point was a small Inuit settlement called Resolute Bay, 1,000 miles from the nearest tree and as far north as you would wish to go. It has been said that, "It's not the end of the earth… but you can see it from there."

The route would take our team across Cornwallis Island, avoiding open water on the land-locked sea ice where polar bears would possibly look for food. From there we would cross the North-West Passage to Devon Island and haul along Jones Sound with a mild diversion to avoid 30 miles of heavy ice rubble coming in from a place that has a sweet-sounding name, Devil's Inlet. The diversion saved us time as we headed towards Gris Fiord from the arbitrary point we named 'Kelly Point'.

At the time only 200 or so people lived in Resolute Bay, and about 80 in Gris Fiord. Some explorers have written indifferent comments about both of these places due to their remoteness, but I admire the solitude and the friendliness and resourcefulness of the communities. I am still in contact with some of them on social media – it is a beautiful area of the planet.

The key to this expedition was that it was the first time I linked directly into classrooms back home. Children would listen to my call through speakers in their schools, and then they would ask the team questions. What a wonderful experience for young minds to interact live with explorers.

To expand on this I then linked up with the ever-charismatic Dr Mark Smith who runs a company called *Contact Engine* (formerly known as *Ipadio*). This collaboration enabled me to take these conversations and instantly post them live to my social media and website. As a result, everyone could have access to that two-way conversation.

It also extended to conference calls, where I could bring in an expert from a different side of the planet along with a child from a school in say, China, with myself in the Arctic. We could then hold a discussion on what we were doing, and then this conversation would go live online for everybody to be able to listen to. It was a great platform to use anywhere around the world, and because it used Iridium satellites, it had better reception than even when I call my neighbour back at home!

Info Point: Kelly Point
A year earlier myself and Mark Kelly had skied from Gris Fiord to this point and then headed back to Gris Fiord again as part of the Arctic Schools Project. The point where we turned round we named 'Kelly Point'. We knew this was a safe route around the ice rubble.

Mark Langridge, myself and Paul 'Vic' Vicary checking our North Pole equipment for the tenth time

What Do You Take?

In terms of equipment, what is necessary and what would be dead weight comes from the experience gained each time on expedition. It's 'sod's law' that every time you are on ice, you wish you had bought an item you haven't got. I live my life generally in a very simplistic way, whether that's on ice or back at home. Preparation is the key to success, especially when it comes to packing equipment.

I have a room at home where I lay out all my items, including both day-time and night-time equipment. I then pack everything in the pulk, take it all out, and then re-pack it again for as many times as is necessary. I have to check the balance of the sledge, as well as the positioning of different parts of kit. If I place my food next to fuel, which has the risk of leaking, the food would then be contaminated and the expedition finished. Some items will need to be taken out first on a trip, so for example the ice screws for anchoring the tent are at the surface next to the tent, which is next to the shovel… and so on.

I will also set out all the food and organise it into calories per day. I look at the food as fuel, making sure that I don't take anything that will not give me vital sustainable energy. For example, if I take a Mars Bar, it's heavy and will only kick into my body 30 minutes after being consumed. The bar will then give me a sugar rush, followed by a quick drop, which is of no use. So I take 5 x 370 calorie protein bars, and 1 x 870 calorie nutrition bar for each day, giving me prolonged endurance.

Clockwise from top left: finished packages of meals the size of tennis balls; Mark Kelly photographs the lengthy process; curry, stew, rice and other hot dried meals with added high-fat products; porridge and raisins with added sugar, honey and dried fruit.

The idea is to pack light. Børge Ousland, one of the greatest Norwegian explorers (and in my eyes the best in the world) advised me to, "Pack light, think ahead, and leave your fears behind." For me, as someone who does not think that he is one of the greatest explorers in the world, I always feel that I need to try harder than anyone else. The way to do that is pack and prepare well before expeditions, keeping it simple and light, and having straight-forward routines so that if Mother Nature throws a storm at me, or a polar bear attacks, then I can deal with it. (I try and keep the same mantra at home, so my life is simple and I can deal with the tough challenges that life throws at all of us.)

I am asked occasionally what is my most important item. Professionally I could not be without a location beacon – that is my lifeline, so if I lose everything I can press a button that will signal that I need to be rescued. This beacon is taped to my person, waterproofed, and accessible at all times.

Before heading out on any expedition I register my journey with the Location Beacon organisation, inform the rescue teams in the vicinity of my start point, and finally check in with the Base Camp team. If I fall into trouble and I cannot contact the Base Camp team, and if I feel it's a life and death situation, I then activate the beacon.

The holding company will receive the distress signal and contact the rescue teams / Base Camp to see if they have heard from me. If they fail to get in touch with me (the beacon could have been triggered by accident), they then send a rescue team to my last known location – which, as mentioned previously, should be in a 10 to 20 mile radius of that point (that's the distance I can physically travel in a day on ice hauling a pulk).

Once, when I was giving a talk I outlined this procedure and somebody said to me, "Scott and Shackleton never had location beacons – you have it easy now on expeditions." I replied that what he said was true, but if they had owned such technology, they would have used it!

Nowadays we have a responsibility to rescue teams, so in my eyes gone are the days of Scott and Shackleton where they would just be responsible for themselves. Now we must consider the safety of professional rescue

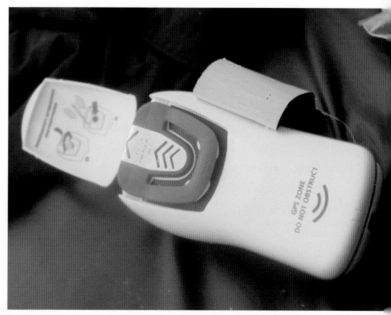

Location beacon to signal for support in an emergency with protective tape to prevent accidental activation

teams who risk their own lives to support our ventures.

Other crucial equipment is eye and face protection – there are so many faces coming back from polar treks cut up with frost nip wounds, so-called 'polar trophies'! It is so important to protect the facial area, and it's also easy to do so. Before the South Pole expedition, Mark Kelly and I had gone shopping in Punta Arenas for something to protect the lower half of my face. My goggles protected my eyes, but I had to find some suitable material that would cover my mouth without affecting my breathing. You can spend hundreds to thousands on expensive equipment, but in this case I ended up sewing a dishcloth onto the back of a wind-proof piece of material, and then attaching this combination to the lower section of my goggles. When it was warm, I was able to lift up the dishcloth like a duck's beak!

Being a naturally warm person, a thick pair of working gloves on top of a pair of woollen 'thinnies' was all that I needed to keep my hands warm and allow me to use my fingers. I have never got on well with mittens during expeditions, because I find them too restrictive. My theory is perhaps backward if I'm honest, as a mitt is better for keeping hands warm. A hand will warm the glove, and not the other way round, so if your hands are cold give them a good shake and allow the blood to flow before putting them in a mitt. The heat from the hand will then circulate inside the mitt, although because a glove has separate areas for fingers this can make it a little harder. I use the same action for climbing in my sleeping bag – I do a little shuffle, warm my body up and then enclose that heat in the bag to generate warmth.

My rule with small pieces of gear like hats, gloves and buffs, is that if you find something that works for you, don't change it. I do test clothing for companies from time-to-time, but it's usually the items I've used for years that work the best.

Boots were different though, and I had taken advice to try a new pair of boots for this trip, which included a toe bar designed to click into the binding. Looking back, this was probably one of my biggest mistakes I made pre-expedition and a schoolboy error. The first thing you tell someone with new boots is to wear them in. My boots arrived really late in the UK and I had nowhere to break them in, apart from around the house walking in and out of rooms with two confused-looking dogs following my every move!

Unfortunately this proved to be a mistake because, as previously mentioned, the binding connection constantly snapped. This ultimately affected my feet that started to fall apart every day as skin began to drop off due to the constant rubbing. One day I took my boot off midday and half of the skin dropped off my left foot, exposing the raw skin underneath. I only had myself to blame for this, and out on the ice I accepted that this was part of the experience of the expedition. I tended to my feet with iodine – I felt like screaming as it hit the raw skin but I held it in (although this was stupid really, as no one would have heard me).

When I skied during the day I didn't feel any pain until I stopped for a drink, when the blood would settle in my foot. I could hardly move through the pain and had to force myself to slowly move forward, like an elderly lady with a shopping trolley – not the professional image I was looking for.

Due to Antarctica being a dry desert, the sores cleared up pretty quickly and within 48 hours my feet were dry again. So in the end the environment saved the day.

Everything I packed served a purpose. I don't carry photos, books or anything unnecessary, although I do have a good-luck item. During the South Pole expedition, I carried a little penguin, only about one inch high. With no music or books to read, each night I would put the penguin out in the tent and often speak to it – "How's your day been?" I would ask. In newspaper reports back home, they drew

A grown man has a one-inch penguin as his only friend!

attention to the similarity with the Tom Hanks character from the film *Castaway* who talked to his ball, 'Wilson'!

Constant rubbing took my skin off

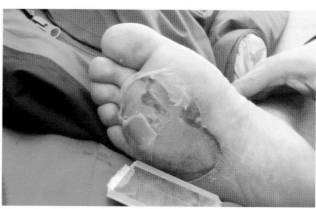
The dry Antarctic wind dried the foot within days

I decided to slow everything down after my drop in morale, re-assessing my progress and taking it one step at a time. I tried to think about the expedition as cold weather camping, not placing too many expectations on myself, and removing as much of my self-applied pressure as I could. The expedition would be more about what I could cope with. I walked away from my static tent one night for about 50 metres and looked back at where I lived – a small tent on a white planet – and took stock of how I was going to approach the next part of the journey. Everything was brought into perspective.

Towards the end of the first week, after an eight-hour trek and discussions with Base Camp about distances, calculations showed that I needed to cover 15 nautical miles a day to complete the expedition in the 50 days I had aimed for – this was still possible. I dumped unnecessary supplies (which were just two bags of Jelly Babies weighing around 5 kg) and ploughed on through heavy winds which often left me feeling frozen to the bone.

When the sun was out I could maintain a bearing by following my shadow, giving me both a sense of direction and of time. When white-outs happened I missed my shadow, saying goodbye to it and then saying hello when it reappeared. With no one around me for hundreds of miles it became a companion to me. The ruff around my hood made a shadow that resembled Darth Vader's helmet, so I managed to keep myself highly entertained! Once I sent an expedition report about this and the newspapers relayed how Darth Vader was with me at the Pole!

The use of real fur rather than fake fur on expeditions is so important. Real fur, generally made from wolverine, will not freeze entirely in zero temperatures and so will keep your face protected from the sharp wind that otherwise cuts into your face like glass. Fake fur freezes, so there is no point in using it in the first place. I hate the idea of fur being used outside of the frozen parts of our planet – there is no need to wear real fur as you do your shopping in London.

Skiing along I was cocooned behind my coat hood, buff and mask – I had created a warm microclimate which enabled me to switch off from the cold and pain. Inside my head I was somewhere else, slipping into one of my dreamscapes as I pushed forward. British explorer Pen Haddow likened his movement to that of a monk – dressed in black with a hood hanging low over his head, his body moving slowly but purposefully. In a good moment you can lock your mind and body into this inner warmth and almost translucent state, allowing you to still stay sharp to any dangers, but also enabling you to cover more ground – it's almost a meditational state.

I suppose it might be the same for a sprinter finally getting into his stride on the track or a marathon runner running at speed with their bodies totally relaxed. It's that moment when everything comes together. However, it also allowed me to think with tremendous clarity about the past.

Selfie at the halfway point

Are You Ever Alone?

*Who is the third who walks always
    beside you?*

*When I count, there are only you and I
    together*

*But when I look ahead up the white
    road*

*There is always another one walking
    beside you*

*Gliding wrapt in a brown mantle,
    hooded*

*I do not know whether a man or a
    woman*

*— But who is that on the other side of
    you?*

> *TS Eliot*, The Waste Land

When my mum first told the family that she had throat cancer, I was absolutely certain that she was going to be fine – this sort of thing didn't happen to our family. The operation she was to have would possibly damage her throat, but it was essential for her treatment.

When I'm asked in talks what is the hardest thing I have ever done, I always think about the moment when I watched the most precious person in my life die of cancer… but for the sake of keeping all things 'expeditions', I usually mention my ascent of Everest or my solo to the South Pole.

The toughest memory I have in my life is this. I held her hand as she was being wheeled through to the theatre to have the cancer removed, an operation which would also take part of her throat away. Mum looked so frail and scared. I kissed her cheek, and she whispered to me words I will always keep to myself. This was the last time she would speak. I smiled at her as the doors closed and told her that we would all be waiting for her.

The next time I saw my mum she was sitting in a chair asleep with a gaping hole in her throat. My brother Rob was at work and although my poor dad was sat asleep bedside her, he wasn't dealing with the situation very well. Mum had her head back with an oxygen mask covering her face, struggling to breathe.

Her beautiful face was all puffy and pale. I had to walk out of the room to find somewhere where I could be alone. Walking to the end of the hospital corridor, I couldn't find anywhere that was private enough for me to cry, so I faced the wall and tried to collect my thoughts.

I lost it. Gripping my teeth and clenching my fists, I tried my best to gather myself together. I broke down alone. I felt helpless and after a few seconds I found a bathroom to wash my face before I returned to Mum's room. She was still asleep, propped up in her chair, and I made a point of looking into the hole in her throat before wiping away some mucous build-up. As on expeditions, I was trying to get rid of the emotion so that I could then deal with the reality of the situation. Later on, when my dad woke up, I was in complete control – I needed to be positive and assertive to support them.

After Mum died just a few months later in 2003, aged 60, family and neighbours seemed curious about how I appeared to be so cold and controlled. In hindsight, I had resorted to using my training to get through the grief without confronting any emotions – I had switched off. I treated the whole process in the same way I deal with any other area of difficulty. I hadn't taken the time out to grieve.

The first time I began to grieve was eight years later on my own in Antarctica. I turned 45 on the 18th day of the South Pole expedition, and Mum's birthday would have been the day after mine, so it was extra special. Out there in the snow I was really missing her.

I am not a religious or spiritual person. However, in some sense I needed to become one whilst trekking through Antarctica to cope with being so very alone. As the expedition progressed I was still heading up a gradient and into strong winds, battling with the elements in order to make ground.

On occasions I gritted my teeth and strained my body as I pushed forward and became lost in my mind, tears rolling down my face with thoughts of my mum. At this moment I felt an arm across my back, gripping my shoulder and edging me forward, leaning in from my left. I sensed a second person speaking to me calmly, "Keep going, keep pushing, you're doing well." I wasn't afraid of this awareness but rather I was comforted by the support.

During the expedition, I felt this same presence about eight times. Sometimes, when I felt I needed this extra comfort, I would call for it… but it didn't come. After the South Pole, when I was heading north to the Arctic, I told Richard Weber about what I had experienced. I felt a little stupid telling him, but he too had experienced something similar on his return leg from the Pole. Searching for a food drop during a white-out, he felt someone on his left-hand side, guiding him to the supplies.

I read once about the last person out of the Twin Towers on 9/11. They had sensed another presence with them. There are many other similar reports throughout history of people feeling guidance. Normally I am pretty black-and-white about life, but I really felt this.

Even if it was as a result of my state of weakness, I felt the reality of a second person.

Whether it was my mum or not, I like to feel that it was her. You never come to terms with somebody close to you dying, but over time I feel comforted to know that she is OK. I feel her sometimes, and it brings a smile to my face.

The pure joy of being on expedition can be seen on my face! The emptiness of a cold world allows your mind to drift to hidden thoughts.

Resting every hour to eat protien foods and hot energy drinks

As the march to the South Pole continued, I had the usual mix of bad luck, inconveniences, surprises, and progress. The usual white-outs hampered my navigation, the bindings on my skis snapped off (fixed, as described, with a little improvised DIY), my body ached from the constant physical punishment, and my feet were a mess of blisters.

Eating three hot meals a day kept my energy levels going. I'm a creature of habit and so I only took six different types of meals with me – beef stew, chicken stew, lamb hotpot, chicken korma, cod with potato, and spaghetti bolognese – with apple and custard as a pudding for good measure. My breakfast consisted of porridge with sultanas. All these meals tasted fantastic after spending the day working for them, although if I had been eating them on a normal day at home they would have taken on a very different taste.

Life in the South Pole is extremely basic. I would eat, move, eat, move, sleep, and eat... and that's pretty much it. The only interruptions were dealing with minor injuries and equipment repairs, usually at night.

The landscape looked almost like the moon's surface, with massive blocks of sastrugi and no animals, vegetation, planes, people or sounds, other than the ever-present howling winds that would beat across the barren landscape. I felt this was as close as I would ever be to becoming an astronaut. (In fact, a lot of training for space missions is carried out in the islands in the Canadian High Arctic, as the surface is similar and the silent remoteness replicates the environment of space.)

Is Global Warming a Reality?

I am no scientist, and neither am I an expert – which is the first thing I admit when I give talks in front of climate scientists! However, through my journeys I have seen for myself the effect that climate change is having on the destruction of the ice, communities whose lives are torn apart by freak weather systems, and unusual animal migration patterns. I have been exploring professionally for half of my adult life, including spending extensive time in the polar regions. I have seen changes for myself and I have spoken with local indigenous people who live on the edge of global warming. I have listened to what they have said regarding the rapidly changing seasons and how this impacts harvests and hunting, which in turn tears communities apart.

I truly feel that when I went into exploration I went in as a student of climate change – almost as an atheist. Yet over the years my views have changed, not just because of my own experiences, but in situations as potentially catastrophic as this, my faith has gone with those people who work on scientific truth. In recent years I have had the privilege to spend time with some of the world's leading scientists on climate change.

There are now enough statistics from 98% of the world's specialists to confirm that climate change is happening, and specifically happening at an increasingly rapid rate within the last 150 years. The question of whether the changes are natural or man-made is beyond doubt.

My expeditions are designed to bring in what I experience and the changes I see into the lives of everyday people. On my own I can do little, but people together can achieve a lot. People change governments, governments make policies, and policies can enable change.

We are already seeing the impacts of climate change on the world, and within a few decades many of these impacts may well be irreversible. In the face of such change, some people feel powerless. My good friend Dr Stephan Harrison is one of the UK's leading climate scientists and over the years has supported a lot of my ventures. I asked him once if the situation was reversible and he replied, "You can't change physics. The point has come and gone were we can make drastic changes, but as long as we keep the level of temperature under a few degrees we might have a chance. We can achieve this by a

Info Point: 'Dr Stephan Harrison'
Associate Professor of Quaternary Science, University of Exeter. His positions include Head of the Climate Change Expert Committee of the UK Government's Office for Nuclear Regulation (2011-2017), Head of the Natural Hazards Risk Committee for UK Government's Office for Nuclear Regulation (2017-), an invited member of the Environmental Research Group and the Climate Research Group of the Institute of Actuaries (2005-2009), and an invited member of the Carbon Counting Group, an international group of economists, scientists, architects, politicians and environmental activists working in the field of mitigation and adaption for climate change (2005).

Open lead with black sea exposed on the 2016 North Pole expedition

massive global effort to decarbonise our energy systems and by recognising the critical importance of biodiversity in maintaining a habitable earth."

My target audience for climate awareness are people who feel that they are detached from the actual situation – it's no good preaching to the converted. One of the major issues we face is how to communicate climate change. If I stood up in a talk and said that there had been a terrorist attack in London that day, then the whole room would listen. Yet if I tried to explain the long-term effects of sea levels rising, then probably most of the room would switch off.

As an explorer, I feel we need to humanise the situation. I do this by showing people how normal I am so they can relate more easily to me. I then go out to places like the Arctic or the Himalayas to develop honest films showing the problems we face on the journeys themselves, not as scientists but as explorers. Once the films are brought back to be edited, we then ask experts like Dr Harrison to add the meaning and truth behind what we have seen.

It's an effective way of educating people to see for themselves the damage and then re-address how they live their own lives to be more efficient. I also discuss these issues in schools, where children seem to be a lot more in tune than adults with the issues surrounding global warming – which is refreshing to see.

When asked whether climate change is really happening, I kind of breathe a sigh of disbelief – are we *still* debating this, or can we just get on with re-assessing how humans impact our planet?

I have been to Dr Harrison's house and met his lovely family. He is a lecturer at Exeter University and is paid at a lecturer's rate; he lives a humble life, and he'll laugh when he reads that he is not a multi-millionaire! He is not driven by money but by *facts*. He is one of thousands of scientists worldwide who all argue that global warming is happening and that changes need to be made. The other 2% of scientists who rubbish these claims are paid by large global organisations who deal with products like oil and gas – their scientists are paid to support the argument that global warming is a con as it will have impact on the profits of the companies they work for.

> *It is difficult to get a man to*
> *understand something, when his*
> *salary depends on his not*
> *understanding it.*
>
> *Upton Sinclair*

Scientists are now delivering alternatives in order to reduce the carbon footprint of the planet – all it needs is for global organisations, governments and for ordinary people to appreciate where we live and to start thinking differently.

During an expedition to the Himalayas, an earthquake hit China and its impact was felt in Kathmandu. After the chaos and the panic settled down, I immediately had a text message from the UK asking if I could meet with Al Gore – within five days! My immediate reaction was yes, but then the reality hit – I needed to get through this devastation to Kathmandu and back to the UK, in only a very short timespan. So began an impromptu expedition where I befriended a high-ranking Nepalese officer who, after I explained my opportunity to talk about climate change (and the issues facing Nepal), organised one of his own military helicopters to take me to Kathmandu. I then had a rapid journey to the airport and a flight back to the UK where I arrived just in time to meet the Vice President of the USA! In the photograph you will see me still in expedition clothing, but all that struggle to meet him for a short period of time enhanced the education programme, inspiring students to understand climate change. Looking back, I wonder how I actually got out of the mountains. Sometimes you need to think past your immediate situation and look at the bigger picture.

Through my own expeditions, if I can build a soapbox for the climate scientists to stand on so that they can make their message louder and clearer, then so much the better. Another reason for me to explore.

Meeting with Vice President Al Gore

The days were folding into each other. Being alone wasn't an issue now – it was positive in the sense that I could make mistakes and not be judged. In fact, over time, each negative became part and parcel of the daily routine experience, allowing me to side-step problematic issues.

When you stare at white all day, every day, for days on end, your senses become so high that the most miniscule change can provoke a reaction. Suddenly in the distance I saw a tiny spec on the horizon. As I moved forward, the image took shape – to my surprise it was a bright orange vehicle which had obviously been heading towards the Pole. As I approached I could see that it was a Toyota Land Cruiser with a tent set up next to it. No one was there, and when I called in to Base Camp I was told that the men travelling in the car had been airlifted back to Union Glacier and would return in a few days, once they collected equipment to repair their damaged vehicle.

Feeling relieved that nothing awful had happened, I pitched my tent right next to the Toyota. In the abandoned tent I saw a tube of Pringles… a temptation indeed, after weeks of eating the same boring food day in and day out. I didn't give in, but felt awkward about snooping around when the drivers of the vehicle weren't there. I sat in the passenger seat, enjoying the comfort of sitting down. I could have slept in the tent and eaten their food, but my polished routine and belief in the balance of life was so strong that the Pringles survived a vicious attack! I slept, and the next morning I moved on, leaving my brief encounter with life behind me.

The abandoned Toyota took me back to an earlier expedition I had been involved in. I joined those responsible for guiding the *Top Gear* team (a popular UK motoring programme on the BBC at the time) to the 1996 position of the Magnetic North Pole. The show's presenters were split into two teams – Jeremy Clarkson and James May headed to the Pole in a modified Toyota, pitted against Richard Hammond travelling with legendary female polar explorer Matty McNair and her team of husky dogs. Matty is a remarkable woman who lives in Iqaluit, a large Inuit settlement on Baffin Island in the Canadian High Arctic. Her children, Eric and Sarah, are also explorers, both having been born into cold weather expeditions. Even their father, Paul Landry, is a legend in the polar world. It was an honour to work alongside such a remarkable family.

The race started from one of my favourite spots, Resolute Bay, and covered over 350 miles of land-locked sea ice moving between islands that sit on the North-West Passage and snake their way to Isachsen, an abandoned town once used for filming *Ice Station Zebra*. It's a haunting location where everything is covered in snow – a great setting for an Arctic zombie movie!

My journey took me to the position of the Pole and back again to Resolute Bay, covering over 700 nautical miles on a snowmobile. If you have never been on a snowmobile it's exciting for the first hour, but then the realisation that you are

just using your thumb to accelerate makes it slightly mundane, especially over such distances. However, the trail was new territory for me so the adventure was there to enjoy.

The Magnetic North Pole constantly drifts, and in 1996 it had been last registered at Isachsen, where the *Top Gear* team were headed. Travelling across thin ice in a heavy vehicle was a nightmare for the team as it encountered fields of ice boulders. Myself and Deirdre, a doctor, both rode a snowmobile each, pulling all the fuel, food and tents on a qamutiik – a large wooden Inuit trailer bound only by rope, but designed to withstand the changing twisting terrain. However, we spent more time digging the vehicles out of snow rather than actually riding on them! Eventually we all made it safely to the Pole location, with the Toyota beating Matty's dogs who, whilst having an advantage through the ice boulder fields, lost ground when on open terrain.

I gained valuable experience of working with film crews and people such as cameraman Simon Wagan who filmed *Touching the Void*, *Planet Earth* and other great programmes. Simon, who had a great eye for filming, was also a down-to-earth person who would share the duties of cooking food and making brews for everybody. It was good to have an insight into the professional way the crew work together to produce stunning footage for a programme watched by millions.

In 2007, when the episode aired on prime TV, my dad phoned to let me know that *Top Gear* were doing a special North Pole race that night. It made me smile as I reminded him I had already seen it first-hand!

The Top Gear presenters, production and camera team and their guides I am on the far left.

I was there purely as part of the support team. As for the presenters, I worked with Richard Hammond first as he completed his week-long training on the dog team with Matty and then spent a further week in Resolute Bay with Matty and myself as we waited for the other two presenters to arrive. I forgot who Richard was after a while, as he just mucked in with everybody – mainly due to boredom. I was refuelling the cookers outside one morning and he stood next to me needing something to do. So he helped for a while and then, together with the doctor, we took a drive across the ice to where some polar bears had been spotted a few days before. The three of us sat in the cab staring out at the Arctic, and as it was soon after Richard's

horrific high speed crash, we both received a first-hand account of what happened to him. I read later in his book that those days waiting to film were probably the worst of his *Top Gear* career… although I don't think that had anything to do with me! I thought he was a pleasant, down-to-earth person.

Through all of his play-acting Jeremy Clarkson was keen to do a great show, which at times put pressure on the experience of the crew. He is the same off camera as he is on, and in a way at least you know where you stand with him. I went to his tent one night as he and James were arguing about how to put it up in what was just a mild breeze. I could see Jeremy was

Jeremy Clarkson and James May pose by their Land Cruiser (the image used on the cover of the programme)

getting cold, so I told him to go to the team tent to get a hot drink and I would help James. He refused three or four times as he stood like a 6'4" boy. I virtually pushed him into the tent and within five minutes, with hot chocolate in him, he was back to his loud opinionated self again.

I heard that he supported a couple of military functions for free – some of the guys from the support team had asked him to do this when he got home – so his heart is very much there, and in recent times I have bumped into him again and had some nice chats about the programme. He's a perfect 'jar of Marmite'.

The presenter I enjoyed the most was James May. Through his grumpy not-wanting to be there attitude, he was at least honest – something that will keep you alive on a polar expedition! Nearing the Pole we camped up for what would be our final night. The crew and the other two presenters went outside to discuss loudly some areas that hadn't been filmed. I was left on my own with James, so I asked him, "Do you fancy a hot chocolate James?"

He pulled out beside him a *Fortnum & Mason's* hamper, opened it up and took out an expensive bottle of port saying, "I've got a better idea, shall we open this?"

As a professional guide in the final hours of approaching the Pole, I needed to do the right thing... it tasted great!

Top: Richard Hammond is joined by the local Inuit children
Middle: BBC cameraman Ben shoots close-ups of the shy children!
Bottom: Testing the vehicles prior to heading out

Filming

If one of the main points of being an explorer is to educate others, then filming what I see and experience is one of the key ways of doing this. The *Top Gear* show is just one of many filming ventures I have been part of. I have been criticised on occasions on why I supported a programme that drove 4x4s across a pure area of ice. Whilst I understand the environmental issue, the bigger picture is larger than just three vehicles. At the end of the day the reason I was brought in was because I had worked in that area for six seasons and I knew the local people, the Inuit guides and part of the route – my presence on the team was based on safety.

On the North Pole leg of the South-North Pole Solo expedition, whilst training in Svalbard, Mark Kelly and I ran into an independent crew working for Channel 5. Their lead, Phil Coates, is an excellent expedition cameraman who himself filmed a remarkable expedition to the North Pole a few years previously. After chatting with him, they decided that the story of my solo expedition was interesting enough to follow. Various problems with this half of the expedition had led me to become more focused on the education and filming side of the trip, and so the timing worked out well. This opportunity to become involved with a television channel would be great for my sponsors, as well as my growing audience.

The crew visited me at night as I camped on my own just outside of the town, and also covered other aspects of the trip. I focused on what I could see while out on ice, what I could hear, how I felt, the fear of polar bears, and everything else I could share along my journey. I wanted people to get a deeper understanding of what it was like out there in the wilderness.

The Channel 5 programme was called *North Pole Ice Airport*, focusing on the landing strip

Inventing the 'selfie' and different ways to capture a solo journey

for the North Pole where people arrive to complete the last degree and other expeditions.

I took my footage and made a shorter film called *Solo Explorer*. It was put on my *Vimeo* channel and the next I heard it had been spotted by an International Adventure film festival. In the end it won a 'best cinematographer of the year' award – this came out of nowhere, and was a complete surprise! It was also later shown on a Sky channel through a company called *Information TV*.

I do believe that you can use social media to your own advantage if done in the correct way. Channels allow you to make your own films without restrictions so that you are able to put your own imprint on them.

Since these experiences, and with the introduction of better and lighter cameras, I have been making documentaries during every major trip. So a film will come out of every expedition, to be used either in TV broadcasts or education. The way that I film becomes very personal, as I am eager that the viewer feels that they are part of the team and can relate to each team member. I therefore take a mix of long shots, to show the remoteness of the environment, and then close-up shots to narrate the drama of the expedition.

And of course, it was I who invented the 'selfie'. During my 2010-11 South Pole expedition, I could only take pictures of myself by fixing the camera to the end of my ski pole. I cleverly hid the actual ski pole from the shot, and it was only the reflection in my goggles that showed that I was totally alone. A year later the whole world was taking selfie photos, and I got no credit whatsoever!

Stills of my 360° film showing nothing but ice – totally alone… and happy

Alone at Christmas. As people at home celebrated I felt so distant from the human race... although I would not have wanted to have been anywhere else at that moment in time.

As I neared the halfway mark of my South Pole trek, I knew that I was making good progress. It was time to start talking to my team back in the UK about plans for my follow-on trip to the North Pole. My mind wasn't really on the South Pole as I transferred focus onto the next leg across the Arctic Ocean.

The next day ended when I made a call to my media team, *Life Size Media*, whilst they were in the middle of their Christmas Party. I had three nautical miles to go, so I sat on my pulk and called into their party.

Over the course of the expedition, including the build-up to the journey, *Life Size Media* (LSM) had done a wonderful job, setting me up with climate change magazines, websites, interviews and a main feature in *Metro* magazine with over 6.8 million readers per day — on Christmas Day the paper had a picture of me on the front cover, setting off from Hercules Inlet, with the caption, 'The loneliest man on the planet'. This picture was one of those taken by the crew on the drop-off plane who then posted the SIM card to Mark Kelly back in the UK — so the idea worked!

It was incredibly heart-warming to hear from the LSM party with their messages of encouragement. As I sat on my pulk surrounded by an horizon of ice, I pictured them all in London celebrating together. I hadn't spoken to some of them in so long and they were all going out of their way to push the story of what I was trying to achieve to a wider audience.

Being out in the vast emptiness, I had little concept of how time was still moving forward for the rest of the world. I felt cut off from reality, but it was a wonderful feeling that only a few people get to experience.

Day 25 was a marker in the journey. I was halfway to making it, and on that day I managed 16 nautical miles, one more than any other day. Using frozen fingers and toes, I worked out that I was managing two miles an hour, and with my feet and skis all in good working order, I was feeling pretty good. If there was a zone to be in, I was in it.

I managed to relax more in the tent and sleep came easily. I could actually feel the bones and muscles just 'let go', and after the bad start to the expedition, things now could not have been going better. I could also feel the fat weight dropping off me, and my stomach felt flat. The only slightly worrying issue was that my legs felt thin with the early signs of muscle deterioration. The next day I pressed on through a five-hour white-out, imagining myself as a single black speck on a white Antarctica canvas – I felt at ease, relaxed and focused.

I tried my best to celebrate with a selection of sweets which I envisaged as a cake

In the run up to Christmas I had spoken to my family. My dad had kept me up to date with what he had seen in the papers about my progress and told me about the front page spread. It was incredibly reassuring to know that people were actually interested in the journey, and I didn't feel that I was alone. The weather on ice was gorgeous, and as the sun's rays reflected on the snow the ice dazzled around me like diamonds.

I spent a lonely Christmas Eve updating my social media sites, sending 'thank-you' and Christmas messages to all those back in the UK. I missed my simple life back home – walking my dogs, going to my favourite café on a Saturday morning and other things that I take for granted.

On Christmas Day, I settled down to my favourite spaghetti bolognese after a tough day on ice. Unknown to me, Dr Mark Smith from *Contact Engine* had put messages from my family and friends together as a surprise for Christmas Day. I was ready to do a standard call, but was greeted by friends at home. The final message came from my niece and nephew, Emily and Sam, and it threw me completely. As I have never had children of my own, they are the closest family I have, and I really missed them at that moment. It was a lovely gesture, but it also played on my mind for four days, to the point that it slightly unbalanced me.

I decided to do something special for the children who were following my expedition. I thought it would be good to do my scheduled daily call but have a special visitor, seeing as it was Christmas. I set the cameras up and prepared some props, such as my wooden cooking board (to make a door-knocking sound) and my map (to simulate the sound of me checking my visitor's route), once I was ready I began the call. Suddenly

My friend John 'the Brush' drew this picture of me supporting a skinny, tired Santa in Antartica

there was a knock at my tent door. When I unzipped the tent, there stood Santa, smiling and calling out, "Ho-ho-ho". He looked skinny and tired from travelling around the world delivering presents, his trousers were covered in soot from the millions of chimneys he had dropped down, and he smelt of reindeer poo!

Santa told me that he was nearing the North Pole, and after I told him that he was on the wrong side of the world, I checked his map for him. Poor Santa, he had made a mistake on the London M25 orbital motorway. He should have taken the M40 junction north but had actually taken the south turn, driven through the Dartford tunnel and then headed down towards Brighton. So I re-directed him and waved goodbye as I watched him disappear into the sky, pulled by a strong team of reindeer… honest.

A funny thing happened later when the BBC asked for clips to use and I just handed over a random file without checking what was in it. Of course the channel used my meeting with Santa as the only footage! I now always check before I send my films off.

The Santa experience was a great way of exciting the children who had been watching my progress over the Christmas period.

I made a call to Santa as he asked for directions home

FREE

METRO

Friday, December 23, 2011   The world's most popular free newspaper

I'll be the loneliest man on the planet

Mark Wood drags his sled across the ice as he embarks on his historic bid to ski alone to both the North and South Poles in back-to-back trips. As the rest of us enjoy Christmas, the 45-year-old will be on his own and into the 35th day of his expedition, described as 'the toughest journey on the planet'

P6-7 »

Media coverage of 'the loneliest man at Christmas'

Origins

As a child I too remembered the excitement of Christmas night and staring up into the stars to get a glimpse of Santa and his reindeers, disguised as comets across the sky.

I was born in the heart of England – in No 118 Hermitage Road, a house in Coventry, practically at the centre of the country. My mum, Carol, was originally from Bangor in Wales, but my dad, Bob, was from Coventry, and they had met in their teens in the local War Memorial Park.

After my dad served in Hong Kong and Aden during his National Service, Mum and Dad set up home together in a simple house where they created a caring environment for me and my brother Robert. My memories are only of a warm loving family – Christmas, birthdays, and holidays are all special memories, and so became strong 'sepia-tinted' moments as I grew up.

Dad spent his working life in car factories around the Coventry area, and Mum worked for the University of Warwick which was very close to our second home and where I spent most of my childhood. They both had a strong work ethic, and although Dad was unemployed a few times and we were often struggling because the factories were on strike, this never worried my brother and me.

Rob was two years older than me, and always had a love of music. Completely opposite to me, he was to become one of the top chefs in the country, cooking for twelve years for HRH The

Mum and Dad in their courting days

Rob my brother (left) and myself struggling with career options!

Queen. This involved travelling with the royal family all over the world on Concorde and the Royal Yacht, cooking for heads of state and presidents, including Nelson Mandela.

I have good memories from my childhood. During the hard winter of 1977 we had a snowball fight at Christmas time with the whole street – even my parents were involved. My love was playing football, and I had trials for Coventry City Boys FC. Dad used to take me to the park and tried to get me to play right-footed, as there were no players in the top league who were left *and* right footed. However, my desire to take this further was never that strong, and so it never happened!

Long-distance running was a passion for me, and for a while I ran with Godiva Harriers in Coventry. I also remember that I had a paper round which consisted of only 27 papers, but which covered a good five-mile route. I did this on my bike, and I guess it set me up for thinking about long-distance journeys!

I recall fantastic family holidays in Norfolk and in Wells-next-the-Sea, where we would hire a caravan and walk through a pine forest onto the beach, jumping off dunes in the sunshine, eating sandwiches tinged with sand and drinking hot coke in the heat of the sun. (I have gone back to those

beaches to train for expeditions and to spend time with my dogs, Poppy and Ciara, and it brings back all those wonderful memories.)

I first went to Ravensdale pre-school before I was six years old. We then moved into a different area of the city where I spent my educational years at Stivichall Junior School and then Finham Park Comprehensive. My favourite subject was art – I had a very broad imagination for the subject and my teacher, Mrs Riley, who believed in me, encouraged it. She helped push me on to 'A'-Levels, even though my exam results were not brilliant, and although she had hopes for me to take my studies further, I eventually chose a more radical route and signed up for the British Army.

Thirty years after leaving school I was jogging in the park where my mum and dad first met when I bumped into Mrs Riley. Even though I was 45 years old, I didn't want to call her by her first name! She is a wonderful person about whom I only have fond memories.

I truly believe your younger days shape the person you eventually grow into. All the different stages of life bring new adventures. I am a lot more comfortable about who I am now, even though I think I could still score the winning goal for England in the World Cup final, or perhaps be the next Leonardo da Vinci!

My First Expedition

I was six when I completed my first expedition! I was not supposed to go past the end of the street, but I couldn't help myself. I had a strange sensation of escapism mixed with butterflies in my belly. With a few coins burning in my pocket I slipped under the hedge and made my way through an alley that eventually brought me to the local paper shop. I bought some penny sweets, so I guess this meant that my first solo expedition was actually supported – but I did make it home safely, which is always important!

Strangely, that first trip is a feeling that I will never forget. I still experience it every time I take my first step into a new expedition. It's an inner feeling of change mixed with fear, and I am always left wanting more. This sense of fear mixed with butterflies in the stomach indicates that a big change is about to happen, and so you need to be alert and prepared for something exciting taking place.

That inner child-like feeling of excitement and escapism is crucial to the whole approach to expeditions.

My first bike which gave me a faster means of escape

One of the great things about kids is the questions they ask… and often they ask the most basic, but also the most important, questions – "How do you keep clean on expedition?"

Heading to the South Pole, I didn't have my first proper wash until day 31. A regular wash is basically a very quick rub down with a couple of wet wipes. On day 31 I boiled some water and treated myself to a 'spa night' in the tent, cleaning myself thoroughly. Having stripped, I was quite surprised at how much weight I'd lost since the start of the journey – it did scare me a bit, as I had thought there would be enough fat to see me through to the end.

"How do you go to the toilet in the extreme cold?" is another burning question amongst children. The fun answer – "Quickly!" The serious answer – if you expose your skin at these temperatures, then there is a real chance of frostbite, so explorers need to understand how fast you need to be when you do 'go'. On the ice, everything has to be systematic and routine, including going to the toilet. Everything you do out there is potentially life-threatening, so you have to treat it seriously.

I remember giving a talk at one school when two little girls with pony tails asked me about going to the toilet in the Arctic, and after answering I added, "If you're not careful, your bum will drop off!" As I walked away their mouths were hanging open.

"Does your pee freeze?" If the air temperature is cold enough, then even the particles in hot drinks will freeze before they hit the ground, so it's possible… although thankfully I've never had this happen to me.

"What is the biggest killer in the cold?" I would say this would be sweat. Moving along we all generate heat, but if you sweat on an expedition it means that you are going too fast. Sweat is fine when you're moving, but when you stop you are literally stopping in a freezer, and that liquid will immediately turn to ice. If ice accumulates around your lungs and heart, you can quickly develop hyperthermia.

The art of survival in the cold is to regulate body temperature. To do this you can take off a layer, allow ventilation, or slow down your movement. However, in the middle of wide-open white space, it can be hard to have a sense of your own speed. So in training the idea is to develop a 'polar plod', a middle ground of speed to sustain yourself but also that ensures that you are covering nine or ten hours of sledge pulling per day. This plod will also make sure you do not sweat excessively.

Snow blindness is also a threat on ice. The sun reflects off the ice and pierces your eyes, so you need to wear goggles at all times. Part of the kit is suntan lotion, and I like to have a tropical-smelling cream with the aroma of coconuts to remind me of being on the beach! Your sense of smell disappears in freezing temperatures, so as soon as you smell something different it intensifies the experience, and becomes an explosion of aromas.

Out in the extreme environments, any small injury that you might think not relevant needs to be dealt with straight away. A small cut on the hand can quickly fester when you're wearing gloves all day long, and if the cut is not treated and becomes worse, before you know it you could become infected, which would have an impact on your whole body.

The most important person on a team is yourself – you have to look after yourself first, as only then can you help other people. It is the same principle when travelling on an aircraft, where the emergency brief advises parents to put on their own oxygen masks before helping their children – if they can't breathe themselves, they are of no use to anyone else!

You are responsible for yourself within a team

Human Contact

With 130 miles to go, I was struggling through a white-out in a field of high sastrugi when I saw tents off in the horizon. I moved towards them, excited but also apprehensive, as my polar trek was supposed to be solo and unsupported. As I pulled closer I stuck my head through the tent to say a friendly 'hello', discovering a six-person team led by Norwegian explorer, Christian Eide. They were sat in their warm tent, wearing t-shirts and playing cards. They looked wind-swept, with red puffy faces resulting from their kite skiing expedition which took them to the Pole and back to the coastline.

I chatted to them for a short while whilst still remaining outside the tent, soaking up the music they were playing – something I had missed since the loss of my iPod! It was lovely to see people again. I had previously met them all at Union Glacier, but after our quick chat I skied a further 3km and set up my tent well away from them. I needed to get myself quickly back in the 'zone' for the push of the final weeks.

I ate my spaghetti again that night before doing my daily binding repair. It had been a strange experience meeting up with them all. This contact, together with the fact that I had been noticing more planes flying along my route to the South Pole, was a stark reminder that the journey was coming to a close.

When I travel I like to think about a familiar route back home with the same amount of mileage. As an example, 20 nautical miles is roughly the distance from my family home in Coventry to my house in Warwickshire. So as I reach six nautical miles on ice I think, well I am now just passing that pub in Kenilworth.

With this tactic in mind and with 130 nautical miles to go, all I had to do was pull my pulk from Stratford-upon-Avon to Brighton!

The weather grew even colder and I had to start wearing an extra jacket for the first time. I had lost a lot of weight, dropping from 106 kg to around 80 kg. During this period I called home and in the background I heard some music. For the next five days I was being driven mad mentally by two lines from the theme tune to the children's TV show, *The Wombles*. They kept playing through my head:

All day long, we'll be wombling in the snow, we wish you a wombling merry Christmas.

It was driving me insane, an annoying mantra that I was even skiing in-time to!

I happened to mention this during one of my daily updates and within a week it made national news in the UK. It was even broadcast on BBC Radio 2 where DJ Chris Evans spoke about an explorer being followed to the Pole by Wombles! The irony was that when I did eventually reach the Pole, there was hardly any news coverage at all – it takes a Womble to make you popular!

Followed to the South Pole... by the Wombles

It's a far cry from Wimbledon Common: Mark Wood is expected to reach the South Pole today – the half-way point in a solo mission to conquer both poles on skis. But he's been haunted by a Wombles tune he heard at Christmas

YOU know what it's like to get a song stuck in your head – especially when you've been on your own for a while.

Unfortunately for polar explorer Mark Wood, the tune he couldn't get out of his mind as he trekked for more than 50 days to the bottom of the planet was... Wombling Merry Christmas.

The former firefighter, who is today expected to reach the half-way point in an historic bid to ski solo to both the North and South Poles, said: 'At Christmas I did ring

by JILL REILLY

my family but afterwards I had a Wombles Christmas song stuck in my head. In the end it seemed like the rhythm of my skiing was even the same as the song.'

What's worse, the 44-year-old, who is unsupported and unaided, lost his iPod on the second day of the challenge, leaving him 'alone with his thoughts'.

Speaking to Metro from Antarctica via satellite phone, he added: 'Most of my kit

is failing, such as my skis – which broke. The weather has been quite bad and at the moment it's a white-out outside the tent.'

From Antarctica, Mr Wood will be taken to the Canadian high Arctic to attempt the North Pole.

When he finally arrives back home in Coventry he will satisfy his craving for a cheese sandwich – and seeing his reflection in a mirror.

Mr Wood is using the polar challenge to highlight the effects of climate change.

Army

With the choice of going to art polytechnic or doing something else, the posters advertising the military caught my eye. I'm not really sure why I joined up, but their marketing worked well on me. I like the outdoors, and I quite fancied the idea of travelling... but that's as profound as it got!

There were five of us who joined up from different areas of Coventry at the same time as me, and all of us ended up being mates. Before joining up I had a full medical on the ground floor of an office next to a large roundabout in the city. As I stood naked with the doctor asking me to look to the left and cough, I noticed people looking in from the Number 15 bus which went straight past our house!

A few weeks later I remember swearing an oath of allegiance to the Queen and then being given an envelope containing £10. Straight away I went to a local record shop to buy the album 'Changes One' by David Bowie, and then I went to the pub with the other four 'recruits'. I signed up for three years with the

Long open runs were probably my only strengths in the army

Second Battalion – The Royal Regiment of Fusiliers – and in the end served four.

Was it exciting? No, it was terrifying. It reminded me of the film *Full Metal Jacket* (which was actually filmed at the barracks I was trained in) and a part in the film where the Sergeant Major comes on to the bus full of recruits screaming at them mercilessly. Over the next 12 weeks we went from long-haired, trainer-wearing boys to shaven-headed, desert boot-wearing men. The training stripped everything away from us – our civilian clothes, our hair, our opinions and identity. We ended up all the same – 35 blank canvasses. We were taught how to use a gun and fight. It was a simple but effective process.

During training I was on guard one weekend, which in normal circumstances was a real pain,

On service with the army

but on this particular weekend Pink Floyd and Eric Clapton had set up in one of the hangars to practise for a world tour. I sat on my own on canvas bags watching them for about three hours as they played songs from 'Dark Side of the Moon'.

After my training I was taken to an almost deserted barracks at Catterick Garrison in North Yorkshire to join my regiment. After a week of scratching our heads, over 600 soldiers returning from duty in the Falklands suddenly joined us. Aged 17 it was completely terrifying – we experienced everything, including bullying. For almost a month no one talked to me as they weighed me up and waited for me to step out of line. I had never been a fighter, and whilst I could protect myself like anyone would if their family were involved, I did not know how to punch. Even now I hear the 'click, click' sound of the lights going on in the barrack room at two in the morning with five or so drunk soldiers standing around my bed, eager to spend a few minutes punching me as I lay helpless. This went on for a few months.

Finally I had enough and stood up to one of them – I punched him as hard as I could in the face, but this just led to a longer group-kicking when my front teeth were knocked out.

I never really felt that I fitted into the military. I was good at the physical side and enjoyed heading out of the barracks on training exercises. I learnt a lot about self-discipline, which included making sure the little things you do can make a difference – such as the simple act of making your bed in the morning or taking pride in looking after your kit. I kept myself in good condition, which helped with the bullying side as they then tended to leave me alone if I could run. It also helped me operate better in harsh conditions.

In the army your life is theirs, and I could not see myself being part of that for 20 years. For me, at that stage of life, the military didn't allow me to be myself. Looking back, if I'd had more knowledge before I joined, I would have been more thoughtful in my choices about who or where I served. I have friends who have made the army their lives and have enjoyed the whole process.

I don't begrudge that time in the military – it's what has brought me to who I am now, and I was proud of being part of a great organisation. During my service we worked for the United Nations in Cyprus, training in Kenya, Turkey, Denmark and Germany. It was certainly four years packed full of experience.

Kenya was certainly a real eye-opener, flying in a helicopter with machine gun in hand across desert plains. We would jump out, and as the helicopter took off and the red dust started to settle, we would look up and see a group of 10 to 15 Maasai warriors walking towards us… pretty scary at the time. Of course there was a massive language barrier, but in the end they came on patrol with us, invited us for drinks in their huts, and shared their lives with us. There I was, an 18-year-old lad from Coventry, suddenly in Kenya with members of the Maasai – it was remarkable, and life was very very different.

In my fourth year in the army I just treaded water, without any clear direction for the future. When I went to sign out to leave the army, the CO (commanding officer) tried to get me to rethink with an offer to be a civilian ski instructor, and also an Arctic warfare instructor course (how ironic)! The army had taught me discipline and shown me the wider world, but in the end it wasn't the life for me… although I had no idea what I wanted to do afterwards.

The Royal Regiment of Fusiliers is one of the oldest and most versatile regiments, having seen extensive tours in Northern Ireland, desert and Arctic warfare, and in the modern era many young soldiers have lost their lives in Afghanistan and Iraq.

Since then I have worked alongside the military on expeditions and sometimes delivered talks about survival to different units. I am assured that the mind-set has changed. Bullying is no longer a part of the set-up, and war is a reality for most of the young men and women that join (as opposed to the idleness I sometimes experienced when we thought that we would never go to war). I have nothing more than pride and admiration for soldiers who selflessly put their lives on the line for the safety of their country.

Poppy and Ceara giving me a reason to come home

Relationships

How on earth is it possible to maintain strong, healthy relationships, when I'm disappearing to the other side of the world on month-long expeditions every year or so, and expeditions that put me at great risk? How do I cope? How does my family cope?

When I deliver leadership talks to businesses, I talk about the importance of having a good home and work life balance. Over the years I have not been very good at this myself, so I really should practise what I preach. Exploration has grown into a passion and I have sacrificed my relationships for this – a flaw within my own character.

However, by exploring the planet and understanding the world, by encountering different cultures and observing our impact on the environment, I believe that I have become a better person. It makes me more aware of my surroundings, and of those I have relationships with. My own weakness is that I never switch off from exploration, so sometimes it can be fairly damaging – it's something I need to address as I progress through life. However, exploration has taught me more about myself, my weaknesses and strengths, and whilst I aim for self-improvement in various areas, I know myself.

It's my dogs that miss me the most when I'm on an expedition. They are a product of the wonderful Dogs Trust, a charity which rehabilitates and finds new homes for dogs which have been abandoned or given up by their owners. My dogs had been picked up (separately) in the streets in Ireland with very little going for them in life. When I leave on expedition I hate saying goodbye to them, and it's heart-wrenching when Pop often looks for me at the door when I go!

All they want to do is give you love and loyalty and all they expect in return is safety, love and friendship. Animals cannot speak for themselves, so it saddens me how humans behave sometimes.

Charlie (my dad's dog), Poppy and Ceara

Cold and isolated

Closing in on the Geographic South Pole

I had spent much of the previous 48 days in fear. Anyone looking at my expedition would have seen this single figure walking across a frozen land. I had coped with the loneliness, the loss of music, the constant winds that brought a sharper cold, the white-outs, and doubt in my own self-belief. I had cried into my goggles at the thought of who was at home and those I had lost during my life – especially my lovely mum.

I felt an inner self-pride concerning the obstacles that I had overcome, both physically and mentally, and with no polar bears to threaten me I had eventually slept well and allowed my body to adapt and grow strong. Stubborn perseverance and persistence got me through most of my hours and it was only now, with a few days left to go, that I realised I could make it.

I truly regard myself as an ordinary person who has to try twice as hard as most people just to succeed. I really felt very proud and knew that I would take these awesome memories with me to the grave. It wasn't ego that made me feel this way, just joy at what I had done.

I spent my second-to-last day trudging through another white-out. Two hours in, and what would break again – my bindings! I had to spend 45 minutes pulling all my bits and pieces out of my near-empty pulk, trying to find pieces of string to hold my skis together. I managed to tie my bootlace around the ski to fix the boot back on. Despite this, I still finished the day with 16 miles behind me. I was seriously hoping that my improvised fix would take me to the end using my skis. The alternative of walking, especially at that late stage with my muscles in my legs so depleted, was not a good option. By now the width of my thigh was the same as my forearm – a thought that scared me for the following trip to the North Pole!

Fire Service

When I left the army I had no idea what I wanted to do, so I put a rucksack on and started to travel. I visited Turkey, worked on a kibbutz in Israel next to the Lebanon boarder, sailed on a felucca on the Egypt Nile and spent my life travelling for over three years – it certainly taught me how to pack light! When I ran out of money I worked in a hotel in London for six months and went running around the Serpentine on days off, so I was able to get my body and my bank balance into a fit state! Life was simple back then.

In my late twenties I thought I had better get a 'proper' job, so I applied to the Royal Berkshire Fire and Rescue Service. Part of the test was mathematics, which I wasn't too good at, so I advertised in the local shop for help. I received some extra tutoring from a retired teacher and I got through the exams and the fitness tests.

> *If you believe it will work out, you'll see opportunities. If you believe it won't, you will see obstacles.*
>
> *Wayne Dyer*

On the surface, working in the fire service looks scary, but you are trained and have all the correct equipment so it becomes a job like any other job – that's what the military and the rescue service has taught me. As a fire fighter you make a proper assessment and act accordingly, calculating the risk. When the bells sound and the adrenalin rushes in, it is exciting, and as a single man with no responsibilities, it was a fun job.

The first incident I ever attended was in Windsor town centre. The changing of the guard ceremony was taking place, the town's streets were packed, and we were called in just down the road to… rescue a pigeon from the top of the Guildhall! As the rookie I was sent up to cut the pigeon out of the mesh trapping it, and I came down with the bird to the applause of a crowd. My friend on the crew was nicknamed Budgie, so for the sake of a good headline, 'Budgie rescues pigeon', we should have sent him up instead.

Of course other incidents would be much more 'dangerous', and you never knew what you would get yourself into with the fire and rescue service.

I enjoyed the operational side immensely, especially the camaraderie, but once I knew how to be a fire-fighter there was not a lot else there for me – the only progress was promotion, by which time I would then no longer be involved in operational duties. Once again, even after ten years, I didn't feel like I fitted in.

I came into the operations room at the fire service one morning feeling that I wanted to do something different, when I noticed an email about someone putting together a team for a polar expedition. I applied, took some initial tests in Wales, and then in 2003 I joined the team for a 70-day High Arctic training expedition.

Following this experience, with permission from the chief fire officer, I began to take three months off a year to carry out an expedition without pay or pension. So for my first four explorations I was still an operational fire-fighter. However, when it came to my fifth expedition, I asked for more time off but the service asked me to take a year out and re-contact them when I wanted back in. Unfortunately, after guiding a team to the Geomagnetic North Pole and then cycling 3,500 miles across America from Seattle to New York, the fire service essentially told me that to rejoin I would have to start from the beginning in recruitment training. I had learnt so much over the ten years of being operational, and I wanted to go back in with all of that experience that I had taken from leading teams on ice, but

they said no. I left the service in 2006, 38 years old, without a job, and all I knew from my jobs so far was how to fire a gun, squirt water and scare polar bears away!

The fire and rescue service was an evolving job, trying to fit in with modern life. I was involved with local and national strikes, walking on Parliament to fight for more pay. Fire-fighters, like most service occupations, are low paid and asked to do much beyond the normal call of duty. They have a high work ethic and always deliver. They are serving the community and making sure it is safe – this is what they are proud of. On reflection, I feel honoured to have been a part of the service.

Leadership

When an expedition is coming to its end, people naturally drop their defences as they hit the home run, sometimes even feeling like the journey has already ended. That's a dangerous time on any expedition. The body is put under so much pressure on the journey, and although the mind may feel relaxed, it is working overtime to focus information every second. When this stops, the danger is that you relax, and this is when mistakes are made. In the military if a patrol is ambushed it is usually on its way back to camp – as the team may feel weak and tired with their minds set on the evening hot meal.

When I lead teams, as I've mentioned already, I always say that I lead from the back. It's not about physically positioning myself behind the team; it's about constantly assessing the team, seeing the full picture which also includes understanding how the team members feel. Everybody has a day off mentally, and that's when they start to judge themselves. I say to people that they would still have bad days even if they were at home, but the Arctic has a way of making people self-critical. When there is little around you apart from endless ice then the focus becomes yourself. So when I'm bringing a team down a mountain, just before we start to descend, I stop everybody and bring the team close together so that they can hear clearly.

With a mild change in voice to emphasise the point, I explain that this is now the time to refocus, to switch back on, because the descent is when mistakes are made. If you maintain a calm level of talking throughout an expedition, then when you need to reinforce an issue, a change in tone works well – you don't have to shout, it's just a change in the character of your voice.

The teachers and children of Sherbourne Fields Special School in Coventry

A good team is usually made up of very different people, all with different ideas. When I select people for a polar team, the first key issue is their personalities, ensuring that I will get on with them. That's not to say that I want comedians or stars, but people who seem naturally able to just get on with everyone else. I am assessing them from the moment I meet them, getting to know who they are, and getting clarity for myself without judging them. However, you never know the true mark of a person until they stand in negative temperatures in the Arctic – the harshness of what they face strips away any pretence they may have and exposes their true self – not many people can deal with this. It's like holding a mirror up to yourself to see who you really are.

Your own personality is a great qualification. When you apply for a job, the interviewers already know about your background and what you want to do, but they want to know about you – you don't have to be loud, you don't have to be quiet, you just have to be you! When I meet people, it is about understanding that individual. Skills can be taught in time but character is so important.

From the back you can see when someone is not performing – it might be psychological, questioning their ability, or it might be physical, not walking at their normal speed. It is down to a leader to then deal with it according to each individual.

Everybody is different, so to have a standard form of communication for every person does not work. A friend once told me that, whilst bringing up six children of different age groups, to get them into the car in the morning, they all needed to be communicated with in different ways. It's the same with a team on ice.

Leadership is something that I have learnt naturally, progressing from being led by others, and then training teams, and now leading teams. Of course I have made mistakes – I'm not perfect. I have worked with so many teams all over the world, and one key thing I do is listen and observe.

I cherry-pick new ideas to try and improve my own skills. I wasn't the perfect soldier, fire-fighter or explorer, but over the years I have learnt to understand myself.

The decisions that I make in the extremes of the planet are parallel to any leadership in the business world. The principles are exactly the same – for example, with a team you need a focus and to have good communication. A leader has to trust their team and allow them to utilise their own skills. They might make mistakes, but they come back stronger. Of course, the flip side to this is not to micro-manage, which does not allow for growth and so does not work in the long run.

You train people to the point of letting them be themselves, letting them bring their own set of skills and ideas to the project or expedition. As a leader you should be seen to be approachable. However, as leader you ultimately make the final decision. If it is controversial, then as long as you have explained why you are making the decisions, it allows people to stay on board. In short, be honest.

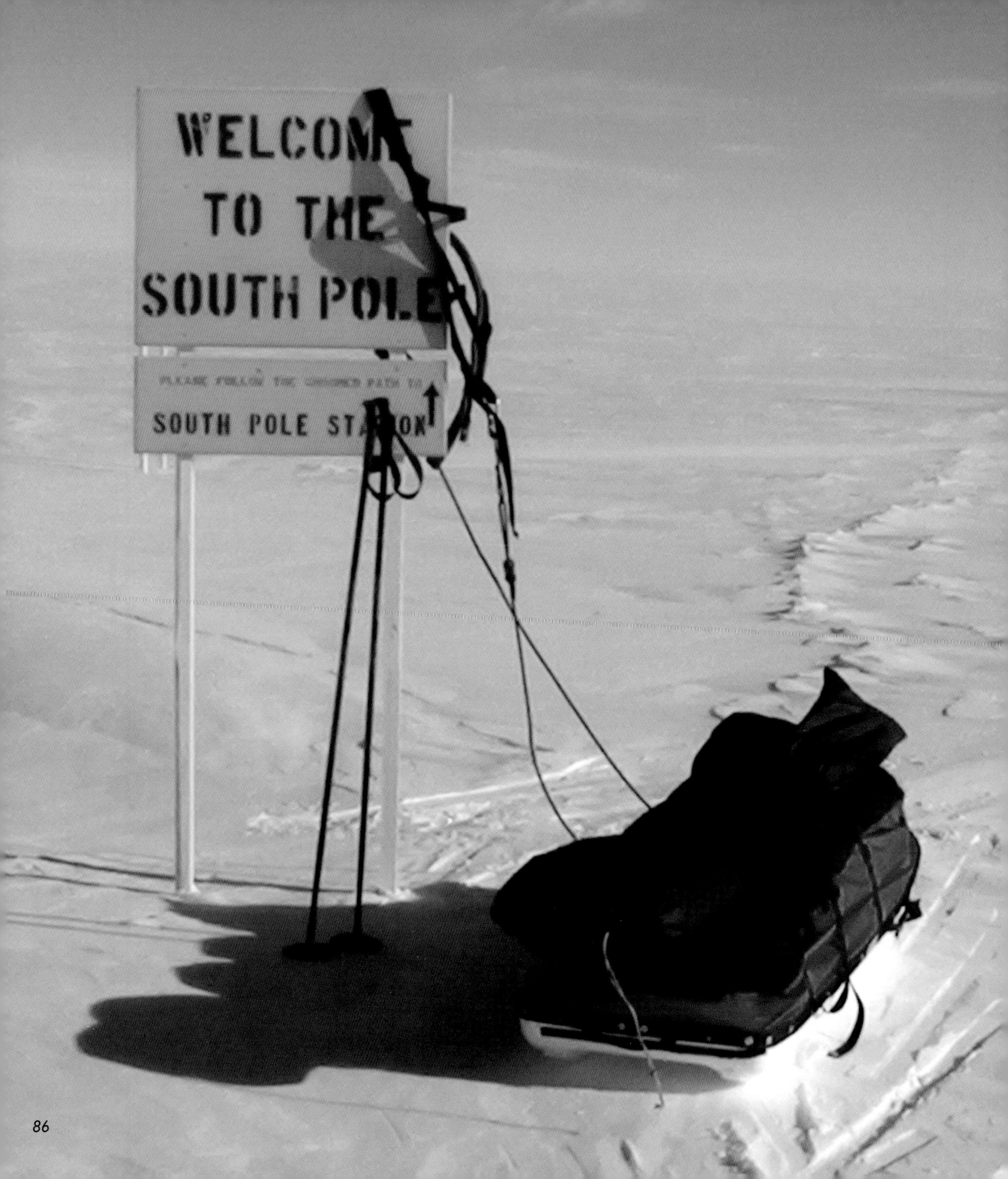
WELCOM
TO THE
SOUTH POLE
SOUTH POLE STA

The South Pole

It was all over so quickly. I woke at 4.30 am on Monday, day 50. I set off and made two calls. One was an early morning voicemail blog to speak to my unknown invisible audience, which on my return turned out to be thousands of students worldwide. The second was to Mark Kelly to alert him of the final hours, but also to thank him for being my eyes and ears on the world outside. Mark had advised me on ideas for enhancing the environmental programme for the journey, along with double-checking that my filming had been done.

I went through cycles of incredible emotions and thoughts that made the day long and hard. As I climbed my final hill scouting the horizon for signs of life, I saw a dark shape. My coordinates were not directed onto it, so it was tempting to ignore my GPS, although this was not the time to be complacent – "Have faith in your equipment, Mark," I said to myself out loud!

My waypoint was a bamboo cane in the ground – so 50 days of ice in a straight line brought me to this bamboo stick, a marker. I literally did a right turn at that point, through a controlled entrance towards the tents in the Amundsen Scott Base, a multimillion-dollar US research complex which stood like a giant space ship. As you approach the South Pole it is a 'clean area', and everyone has to collect and carry their own human waste in special bags, which are ultimately flown back to South America to be disposed of. The marker exists so that you are not walking all over the research area. It would have been quicker to ski direct, but like walking across the grass on a military base, you don't know who is watching you!

Arriving at the Pole

Those final few hundred yards drained my whole body. I had been so tense that my mind and body suddenly decided it was okay to relax – but it wasn't. I needed to drag my pulk just a little further. After 612 nautical miles (700 statute miles) I arrived right on schedule – the last few miles had been really tough going, and it had felt like I was pulling a truck behind me instead of a much lighter sledge!

When I arrived, Mark George, an Australian explorer, met me at the door of the tent and gave me a big hug. Mark had been the very last person to shake my hand and wish me well 50 days previously at Union Glacier – Base Camp. Human contact felt unnatural. He handed me a bottle of beer as I walked inside, leaving my battered skis and pulk outside. It happened to be the 100-year anniversary of Amundsen's arrival at the South Pole, so a tent had been set up for visitors – and I was a visitor!

I felt wobbly inside the tent – I think my body was in shock. I looked around at the faces that greeted me, other keen explorers who had in their own right completed extraordinary expeditions, but who still had the strength and kindness to clap as I stood in front of them. I felt humbled and a little embarrassed. A familiar face was Eric McNair-Landry, who was on an epic kite ski journey with British explorer Sebastian Copeland, and it was at this point that I met my next inspiration in life, Henry Worsley. He came into the tent and shook my hand. His expedition partner, Lou Rudd, also came up and they both sat with me. They had both completed an epic expedition covering the footsteps of Captain Scott, while the second part of the team were covering Amundsen's route as part of the British Army's 2011/12 Centenary Expedition to the South Pole.

Mark, Henry, myself and Lou

I had an instant connection with all these guys, all like-minded people sharing the euphoria of a completed expedition. The administration team at the South Pole gave me a great meal, but because my stomach had shrunk so much, I couldn't eat it all. That's when I really made friends with Henry and Lou, when I shared my food with them – and that's when we truly started to gel well!

On refection, I also felt sad. Even though the journey had been so tough, it was one of the most incredible times in my life, and it was now over.

Amusingly, I was about 500 metres away from the ceremonial South Pole where explorers stand to have their final photos taken. The guys in the tent asked if I was heading down there and I answered that I would just rest up and socialise for a while – perhaps I would go down tomorrow to take photographs. I did not realise that actually *touching* the Pole was the final step, and now in the history books the trip is recorded as a 51-day expedition, which is funny. However, for me the journey was the main part, and reaching the Pole was just a means to an end – and every journey needs an end.

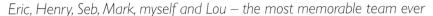

Eric, Henry, Seb, Mark, myself and Lou – the most memorable team ever

Communicating to the World

As I have discussed, one of my key reasons for exploration is to educate and inform – and unless I have effective ways of doing that, it becomes fruitless. One of my major sponsors has been Skype, where some of the key personnel from 'Skype in the Classroom' (Jonathan, Jacqueline and Andy) have believed in what I have been trying to achieve.

They had seen the need to connect with schools from remote areas of the planet, and the obvious opportunities for Skype. I worked closely with Skype on new projects within the Himalayas as they backed the idea of the Global Schools Project. Whilst on a trip to Everest, I had visited a few villages *en route* and spoken to the locals about supporting them in some way. They suggested that the schools were in need of equipment and teacher support. With funding from Skype, I then led an expedition to take computers, screens, projectors, sports and other learning equipment up the mountains. Roof-mounted solar panels provided sustainable energy, and a small cyber café built for trekkers fed money back into the schools to support maintenance of the equipment.

Our journey transporting the equipment hit some pretty bad weather and we had to walk over very rugged ground to reach these schools. At one point some of the equipment slid down the side of a mountain, but the determined porters, who had carried equipment on their heads for days, would not give up – they slid back down to retrieve the load and to make sure

Technology allows me to speak directly to students from anywhere in the world

91

everything arrived safely. They were equally thrilled at helping local children become connected. It became a joint project with the Nepalese teams led by my friend Devendra Rai and my own team of explorers, teachers, film crews and climate scientists.

From this trek, Devendra and I developed the Global Schools Programme which built education initiatives into future expeditions.

I advertised for people to go on treks to Mount Everest Base Camp, and as part of their journey the trekkers (a mixture of students, volunteers, teachers and others) were involved in setting up the project. I will always be grateful for their enthusiasm and support, and I felt rather emotional when I saw them painting a school and setting up all the equipment.

On the South Pole trip, I used Skype to connect with schools around the world before and after the trek itself, bouncing on my reports via satellite phone, and speaking to thousands of students when I reached the mainland. Many came up with their own ideas and questions, and described projects they had been working on to link with my expedition. These students had followed the route daily as it progressed, and for them to be able to chat with me afterwards was exciting.

This all happened because Skype believed in me.

To strive, to seek, to find, and not to yield.

Tennyson, Ulysses

One of the most important lessons I have learnt about the end of an expedition is the huge transition required when returning to civilisation. A little awareness of this goes a long way with other people you meet!

I remember a few years earlier when I had observed a small team of marines during a training expedition in the Canadian High Arctic, and how they had arrived at our training ground having spent the last six weeks out on ice. They were scruffy, smelly and had grown rough beards. Looking rather intimidating, they sat down and made tea and toast, which they then humbly proceeded to offer to the others in the room. This act spoke volumes to me on how to conduct yourself when you step back into civilisation.

And now, at the end of the South Pole trek, I was acutely aware of how long I had been away from human contact and I had to remind myself about my appearance and how to behave amongst people again. One of the more bizarre traditions at the Geographic South Pole is overfeeding new arrivals. I'm not entirely sure if this helped, as my stomach had shrunk to the size of an orange. There was so much food that went to waste as I was given salmon sandwiches, cheese, grapes, beef stroganoff and so much more. I slept like a baby that night – and in the morning it felt strange not to be packing down my tent to head out over the ice.

My taxi home

I had to wait six days before I could get a flight back to Union Glacier on 13th January, and then on to Punta Arenas six days later. There were eight of us waiting for transport, but we all got on well, sitting around a table sharing meals and our experiences – and making tea!

As I have mentioned, Henry Worsley was with a team of five serving soldiers, retracing the exact routes used by Scott and Amundsen in 1911, crossing 900 miles in two months. Henry had recruited serving soldiers from all areas of the army, marines and parachute regiments. During the year they had taken time out from their own units to train together for their extraordinarily inspiring expedition. Worsley's body and face were in bits, but being the soldier that he was, he and his team had struggled through.

Henry himself was a Lieutenant Colonel in the 22 SAS Regiment, a quiet, unassuming and easy-to-get-on-with kind of guy. One hundred yards from the South Pole, we would spend hours just sat at the table chatting in the main team tent.

Over the six days of waiting for a plane to pick us up, humour and stories of the past kicked in, as well as ideas for the future, and we created a bond. Of course I was headed for the North Pole, and as I was about to get on the plane (Henry was waiting at the South Pole for his Amundsen team to arrive), Henry pulled me to one side. We both walked a little way from the plane and he wished me luck with humble words of encouragement which really resonated with me.

After the expedition, when I returned to London, I met with Henry again for the final time; we met up in a small café near where he lived. He brought me a copy of his book which he signed for me, and he also wrote the following words that I will cherish for the rest of my life:

> To Mark,
>
> A chance encounter at the South Pole in January 2012 has paved the way for a lifelong friendship… which is far more important than reaching 90 degrees South.
>
> Henry Worsley

In return I gave him a bottle of Shackleton whisky in a presentation box. Over a cup of tea, we swapped stories and ideas. Henry was an incredible soldier and explorer, but also an amazing family man. For the very short period of time I knew him, he was an incredible friend.

Very sadly, Henry died in 2016 while attempting a solo unaided crossing of the Antarctic – following in the footsteps of Sir Ernest Shackleton. When we heard the news that he had passed it was tremendously sad. I met his wife and son about eight months later and chatted to his son about the two occasions I'd met his dad. I could see in him all the strengths that Henry had possessed.

We are the Pilgrims, master, we shall go always a little further:
It may be beyond that last blue mountain barred with snow,
Across that angry or that glimmering sea.
White on a throne or guarded in a cave
There lives a prophet who can understand
Why men are born: but surely we are brave
Who take the golden road to Samarkand.

James Elroy Flecker
The Golden Journey to Samarkand *(1913)*

Amundsen-Scott Station

The Amundsen-Scott Station is a permanent US research base located at the Geographic South Pole, the southernmost place on earth. Located on an elevation of 2,835 meters above sea level, it has been demolished and rebuilt several times since its original construction in 1956. It is the only building in the world where the sun beats down continually for six months of the year (not counting white-outs), which means that for the other six months of the year there is complete darkness. There is only one day and one night each year.

The insides of the station resembled a space ship, with long metal corridors leading off into various rooms. There were greenhouses growing vegetables and herbs, and a music room set up with guitars and drums. The Amundsen-Scott Station accommodates up to 250 people and was built for the scientific community. With such luxuries as a basketball court, a gym and a restaurant, I felt they were well taken care of during the long winter months whilst they were stranded in the middle of nowhere – something that appealed to me!

After 50 days on ice, sitting on a clean toilet with a porcelain seat was 'heaven on ice'! When I looked in the mirror and lifted my shirt, I saw my ribs for the first time in 40 years. I'd lost over 29 kg since leaving Union Glacier, and would need to replenish my body stores before commencing the North Pole trip.

50 days on ice took their toll

Twin Otters, my entry to and exit from the wilderness

The North Pole

The intention of the expedition had always been an attempt to become the first person in history to ski solo, unsupported and unaided, to both the Geographic South and the Geographic North Poles consecutively.

Reaching the South Pole was only the first half. Within days of completing that part of the expedition, and having lost a lot of body weight and mental strength, I would leave the ocean's coastline in Canada at Cape Discovery and cross over broken sea ice to arrive at the North Pole – all within 65 days.

During my time at the South Pole, I had been relying on the team I had built around me in the UK to ensure that the money required for the North Pole expedition would be ready in time. After being flown back to Union Glacier, I flew to Ottawa in Canada to begin the second leg of my journey – but by the time I got there, frustration set in as the plan began to fall apart. The company that was to fly me in and be on standby should I need rescue wanted £100K transferred into their bank as a guarantee fund. Although I explained my years of experience, they remained unconvinced about my solo trip (partly because their fingers had been burnt on a previous incident with another solo attempt when the person had been rescued but did not end up paying the rescue company – so not only did they risk their own lives, they lost a lot of money as well). This individual not only had an impact on my plans but over the years he has also had a negative impact on other teams hoping to head north on ice.

The formidable risks these pilots subject themselves to by landing on open water sea ice is alarming and, naturally, their organisation had a responsibility to reduce this risk as much as possible.

My pulk with all my kit and provisions... I've never been a colourful person!

Left: tent, drinking bottle, snacks.
Right: sleeping mat, cooking equipment, sat phone.
Top: rifle.
Unseen: food, fuel, spare clothing... and tea-bags.

Open water training with Richard Webber

I was in Ottawa to start my open water training with Richard Webber, as part of the preparation for the North Pole run. I had several sessions dunking myself into the frozen lakes wearing an immersion suit and safety line, but during this transitional period I spent most of the time trying to fix up another route to the North Pole. I was desperate to complete the planned expedition, as I felt I had a responsibility to all the students following me, as well as to myself.

I had gone up to Canada with the idea that the team in the UK had raised sufficient funds, so this additional £100K seemed impossible within the short amount of time, especially as I was having to negotiate with sponsors so far away from home. I was desperately trying to raise the funds on the internet and phone whilst in Canada, but it was virtually impossible. In my mind I had successfully completed the South Pole leg and thought I had the funds for the next leg, so this was a real mental blow to me at the time.

Reluctantly I returned to the UK, and although my main sponsors agreed to underwrite the costs if something did go wrong with the North Pole trip, the airline company was not convinced. Appeals for funds in the limited time available failed.

It's difficult to put into words how I felt – three years of putting the expedition together, succeeding on the first leg of the journey where many thought that I would fail, to then be faced with an expedition collapsing in front of me. I respected the Canadian team's decision, but to be able to live with supposed 'failure', you need to make sure you have done everything you can to succeed. Only then can you understand the process clearly and live with the consequences.

The most important aspect was to fulfil the education programme for Skype and to put a cap on the expedition. The option to reach the top of the world was still there. I decided to attempt the journey via the Norwegian route to the Pole – and so the expedition was reduced to a solo from the last two degrees to the North Pole.

My home on ice

Am I Crazy?

I remember once how someone who worked for the BBC had been shocked at how dangerous my 'job' was. However, I disagreed. In the military and the rescue service, you know what you are getting into, and you can prepare. Similarly, in exploring you also have a good idea of the risks involved, and so you can prepare the equipment, you can train, and you can focus for the trip. So because of this, I do not feel that what I do is risky. Whilst the psychological strain of a tsunami or a terrorist attack cannot be planned for, expeditions can.

Of course, there is also a sheer determination to fulfil the goals – there has to be – but I have to give clarity of thought to anything that changes throughout any expedition. And the biggest fear for an explorer in a moment of stress is finding a reason to give in.

The first time I went to the Arctic in 2003, I flew into Ottawa where the temperature was -35°C and snow was piled up against the windows as we sat in the warm cafés drinking fresh coffee. From there we flew a further ten hours north. The planes we travelled in were getting smaller and smaller, the people and clothing changed, and we started to see the Inuit people and Canadian construction workers. We landed at the airport in Resolute Bay (along the North-West Passage, 78° north) and stepped into -35°C with strong winds. I was petrified, knowing that we were going to spend 70 days there. I started coughing due to the cold air in my lungs. As I stood in the white void I felt frightened and claustrophobic. (The feeling of claustrophobia is not being able to get out of that situation, whether you're in a closed lift or in an open never-ending space.)

However, eventually I learnt not only how to live on ice and survive in those conditions, but most importantly I learnt how to appreciate the environment I was working in. The adrenalin rush, the adventure, then became a drug, almost a life addiction.

Resolute Bay

North Pole Setbacks

Arriving in Barneo Ice Base, I was faced with similar troubles. The camp is sponsored by the Russian Geographical Society and has to be rebuilt every year due to northerly winds which cause the camp to drift in a south-easterly direction at a speed of 0.8km/hr. It's a mixture of tourism and scientific research, a destination for people doing expeditions, whether by skis, sledge or dogs, and is built from a series of specially designed tents for Arctic conditions, all connected to the main mess tent and heated to a temperature of between 15° and 18°C.

Arriving a little after 6.00 pm, I had a mini-panic as the person doing the flight manifest scrolled through the page unable to find my name. After a minute or so, he shouted over to the rest of his team, asking if any of them knew of a 'Mr Grant Thornton'. It was a huge relief as I finally realised that having the name of one of my sponsors all over my jacket had caused some confusion!

I received another lecture from them about how dangerous it was to attempt this expedition on my own. Memories of Punta Arenas came flooding back as they looked at this unknown ordinary person in front of them.

There were two teams at the base who were being led by individuals I knew from previous trips: Doug Stoup, the great American explorer who had told me to immerse myself in my South Pole expedition as quickly as possible, and Alan Chambers, a British explorer who led the first British team to travel from the coastline of Canada to the North Pole – one of the good guys of exploration. All three of us sat around a small table in the briefing room about to be 'talked at' by the Base Camp operator and Russian explorer Misha Malakhov.

There were also TV cameras on site filming the pre-expedition meeting for a Channel 5 programme. Misha informed us that we would be leaving in half-an-hour and he pulled out maps to explain the route and weather conditions, as well as the ocean-drift and why they were putting us on the ice at that time. Misha had gone with Richard Weber on a North Pole return journey in 1995, so he was a well-known and respected man in his profession. Unfortunately, he treated me as if I was a complete novice.

After the meeting and in front of the cameras, he suggested that I join Doug and his team because he had some serious concerns about my solo attempt. In actual fact he was about to suggest to me that I join the other team, but I said to him, "I know what you are going to say, but it's not going to happen." Without Mark Kelly there to help me keep a cool head, I quickly became agitated. I was dealing with the stress of not leaving from Canada and being reduced to the last two degrees, and then someone was telling me that I couldn't even do a solo. And whilst all this emotion was going on, a TV camera was being pointed at my face! I explained to Misha that I had just completed the South Pole alone and knew the Arctic as well, having completed 14 major expeditions, but this seemed to have little impact on his opinion of me. At that point I needed to walk away from the situation and calm down.

After a very short while outside I came back in and the TV crew wanted to interview me. I said that I respected Misha and I understood that he was only concerned for my safety, but he didn't know who I was. As soon as they put the camera down I added, "But he soon will" (although the actual words were a bit harsher). The cameraman quickly lifted his camera again and asked me to repeat myself... but I didn't!

Further to Misha's concerns, they unzipped my pulk to check it in front of all the other teams, who with respect were novices. My equipment was super light, efficiently packed and practically perfect, but they were still reluctant to let me go. I almost had to fight for my position on the helicopter. My frustration again was so high – from the very beginning of this project three years earlier, I had experienced people saying that I couldn't do it, and even now when I had my final steps to take, it was happening again.

As the helicopter flew me over the frozen ocean, I could see incredible shifts of ice with open water leading all the way back to the Pole – my heart sunk. I could now understand why the camp manager had been so reluctant to let me go out alone. The unusual amount of open water would make the journey a lot more dangerous than the South Pole.

I spotted dark clouds over the horizon, an indicator that open water lay underneath them. On previous expeditions I may have only seen one or two such clouds, but these were everywhere. The sea ice didn't look that flat either, appearing to be more of an obstacle course with ice sheets running off into the distance. The familiar feeling of fear sat inside of me. All I wanted was the helicopter doors to open so that they could let me back out into the freezer.

Back on Ice

It was 1.00 am by the time I reached my drop-off point and the temperature was a pleasant -25°C, so I was feeling pretty toasty in all my gear. The crew dropped my pulk off and I lay down on it as the helicopter rota blades began whipping up the snow into a mild blizzard. Under the noise, the helicopter disappeared. I lay still for a few more moments. As I opened my eyes, I stared up at the sky where the 24-hour light made me squint. I took a deep breath and felt my body relax. No more people. No more doubts. Just alone again in the cold. A smile came back onto my face for the first time in weeks.

I decided to camp because I was tired. I had time on my hands and I needed to take the stress of the last few weeks away. I sat in my tent with a hot chocolate and a beef stew. I let the cooker burn for a while to warm the tent up a little. Before zipping up my sleeping bag I took a last 360 degree look outside – I was now in polar bear country, so a new obstacle had been added to the list. My gun lay half in and half out of the tent, just by my head. It would rust if it was inside, so leaving the metal parts outside made sense – it needed to be in arm's reach of where I slept.

The contrast between the Poles was huge. When I set off the ice was wide and very open, but I soon started hitting lots of ice rubble – more like slabs of ice. The ocean movements had created high ridges in the ice which I had to weave between, dragging my kit behind me.

Russian helicopter replaces Canadian Twin Otter

Snow often builds up on the ice rubble and can be lethal when not using snowshoes or skis. I came across four or five frozen leads which were about twelve foot in diameter. Although some water had leaked through in various places, I tested them with my ski stick and then carefully walked over them, pulling my pulk behind me. At -28°C it was very cold. At times the cloud would cover the sun and so the temperature dropped considerably, although this felt good because my body could then work harder without sweating too much. Being in the North Pole made me much more aware of the impact of changes in the climate.

The temperature difference between the South and the North Poles was very distinct. The South was extremely windy and exposed, but also dry, and on occasions warm. The North felt like a wet, sharp, cold – the kind of cold that gets into your bones – due to the ocean below my feet.

On the second day of my North Pole run, I came across incredible amounts of open water. Based on what I knew, this was most unusual. It can be extremely difficult to assess your route on the ground, as you've no real idea of what you're walking into. Watching for changes to the ice colour and the effects of the ice rubble is about all there is to help gauge the safest path – other than using my ski stick! My sledge became caught in the water a few times, but it was no great effort to pull it free. My mind was working overtime, unlike during the South Pole leg where I drifted off on many occasions.

There was just so much frozen rubble everywhere, some of it the size of cars. The rubble is formed when the movement of the drift below cracks the ice, creating boulders which then form an ice wall. It makes great filming, but it also slows the journey down.

Each night out in the Arctic as I slept, my tent would naturally drift another one mile closer to the Pole. Thankfully on this leg of the expedition I had the benefit of a new iPod, so I could listen to music at times, which really helped motivate me as I trudged through the rubble. (I would listen with just one earpiece in, so that I could still be alert to any possible dangers, such as polar bears!) After 50 days without any entertainment in the South Pole, it was great listening to music that I hadn't heard for so long.

'All the Young Dudes' (David Bowie), 'Doing Nothing' (The Specials), 'Live Forever' (Oasis), 'One Day I'll Fly Away' (Randy Crawford) and 'I Know' (Dave Pilla – Dave is a busker in the UK but also does a lot of music for my documentaries) – I enjoyed these tracks and many others set against the backdrop of a frozen moon.

There is no greater drug than listening to 'Comfortably Numb' by Pink Floyd as you stand alone at the North Pole.

The shadow proves this was a selfie

Polar Bears and Penguins

It's an understatement to say that my South Pole journey had the benefit of no night-time anxieties about polar bears. Polar bears really do put an edge on to an expedition. They are circumpolar in distribution, inhabiting the majority of Arctic seas and coastlines. They range across territory owned by Canada, the United States, Russia, Sweden, Finland, Norway and Denmark. There are an estimated 20,000 to 40,000 polar bears remaining in the wild. The United States Alaskan population is thought to number around 2,000, while Canada's polar bear population is estimated at between 13,000 and 15,000. Polar bears are the largest living land carnivores, with males reaching a weight of up to 650 kg (1,433 lbs) with females weighing up to 250 kg (551 lbs).

On the North Pole leg of the expedition, the nights were not as peaceful because the danger of polar bears was very real. After my long cold camping trip in the south I really did need to switch on to the new environment of the Arctic Ocean.

However, as dangerous lists go, the bear is further down on the list after open water, thin ice, minus temperatures and the ever-changing shifting sea ice. As the ocean moved below, the ice would drift, so the environment was unpredictable and unforgiving.

As part of my routine, each evening I would check my rifle, flare gun, pen flares and pepper spray to make sure everything was intact and in place for the night ahead. Light was one advantage I had. In mid-March the summer solstice kicked in and so light would not define a day, although the temperature still seemed to drop during the night-time – which would help if I needed more hours for skiing towards the end of the trip.

I would inspect the rifle for a possible build-up of ice in the barrel, and then I would cock it without the rounds to make sure that the working parts were not sticking. I wouldn't put a round in the barrel, but the safety catch was always off. This was to create a physical act of loading at the point of firing, and also the safety catch could possibly freeze in the 'on' position – which to state the obvious is not good!

The rifle was positioned just by the tent entrance, with the butt sticking into the tent and nozzle sticking out. I generally put a small bag over the nozzle to protect it from any spin drift (light layers of fresh snow spinning across the ice as it's blown by the wind).

In truth the point of having a rifle is as a last resort, or as a last line of defence, to kill the bear. Sometimes you can fire towards the foot of the bear, if the distance is good enough, hitting the ice or snow which will then spray over the bear in an attempt to scare it away.

On one occasion on a previous training expedition I fired over the top of a bear. However, it didn't react to the loud 'crack' in the air because it hears this every day with the cracking of the ice.

A flare gun can also be used, firing at the feet of the bear or high above it. This creates a large visual red firework blast and often does the job. The best form of bear-scarer I have found is a pen flare, a very technical piece of equipment – a pen with a flare on the end! You aim it in front of the bear, and when it explodes like a small firework it generally scares the bear away. On one occasion I triggered a pen flare at a bear but it bounced on the ice in front of the animal, much like skimming stones in the water, and it went over the top and exploded behind him. The scared bear then came running towards me whilst looking directly behind at the red flare. I would love to write about how professional I was, but it was more like a black-and-white slap-stick comedy, as the bear ran straight through the camp!

I have seen over 20 bears during the course of different expeditions. Male bears will operate alone, but in March and April female bears come out of semi-hibernation and usually walk with their cubs – hence why they are the most dangerous, as with any animal a mother will always move to protect her young. There is another advantage I have had in seeing bears. In the areas that I have operated in, polar bears generally have not seen humans before, and so they are simply inquisitive about our smells and colours – they want to know about this new 'animal' in their home environment. So with this I have had time to react….

My initial reaction is to monitor the bear, taking photographs and being aware of where they are and what they are doing, whilst always being alert to the fact that I might need to scare the bear

Close quarters with an inquisitive polar bear

away. This is usually at a distance of over 150 metres. After this you need to make sure they are scared away, because if they are not they might leave but return a few hours later. On route to the Geomagnetic North Pole in 2004, we crossed Ellesmere Island in the Canadian High Arctic, heading though a trading route from Greenland to the northern territories of Canada called the Sverdrup Pass (named after its discoverer, Otto Sverdrup, Norwegian pioneer of polar exploration). A bear spotted our team and stayed with us for three days, stalking us from afar. We put in night watches and thankfully it eventually moved on.

If a bear becomes familiar, it will eat your food first, trash your equipment and then think about you as dinner! If you are forced to shoot a bear to protect yourself, you are required to register it with the nearest environmental rangers who will investigate to ensure a criminal offence has not been committed. If the bear is more than 200 meters away, then really you would have had enough time to scare the bear away rather than kill it.

There was a well publicised incident where a team of students were attacked by a polar bear and the animal had been shot. Afterwards, during the investigation, the stomach of the bear was opened to reveal it was empty. The bear also had a mouth full of blackened rotten teeth. He was sadly deranged and hungry – the investigation was extensive because one of the students had been killed and others sustained terrible injuries. As the bear was in such a bad state, I believe whatever safety technique the team might have used, the bear would have probably attacked anyway. It was famished – something which of course can be related to the change of climate and how polar bears are moving south… and so encountering more humans. Some think that bears will survive on land, but they require a high level of protein, and so hunting seals is vital for their diet.

They are beautiful and majestic animals, and seeing bears during an expedition adds a certain something to any account of a trip to the Arctic. They can run as fast as a horse, are incredibly clever predators, and their sense of smell is acute, which is extremely important in detecting food sources – polar bears are able to smell a seal from a distance of more than 32 km (20 miles). They are one of the most wonderful creatures I have ever encountered.

Sadly I have not seen any penguins on expeditions. On the South Pole trip my route took me inland where there was nothing living… except for me! However, about 25 miles away from my house in England, there is a penguin sanctuary, proving that you don't have to go too far to explore!

Info Point: 'Polar Bears'
The only time polar bears do something resembling hibernation is when a female polar bear makes a den in which to give birth and then take care of her cubs. Other than this polar bears remain active throughout the whole year. However, during the winter polar bears enter a state which is known as 'walking hibernation'. During this period polar bears are able to maintain their body temperature while reducing their metabolic rate and re-cycling proteins. They usually enter this state in the winter because this is when food is scarce.

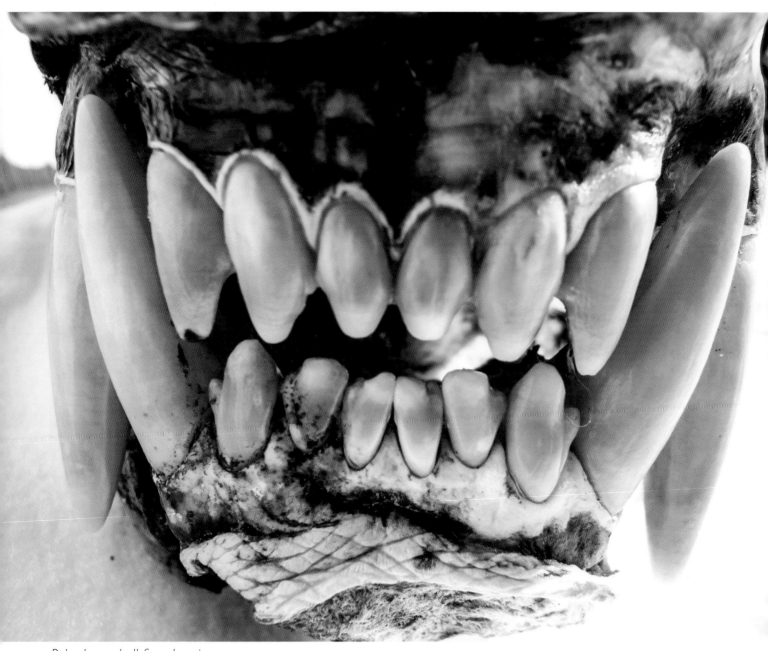

Polar bear skull found on ice

The third day of the North Pole leg began with a white-out and the temperature was absolutely bitter. For the first time I put on a second jacket, but the chill still went straight through my legs. I came across lots of giant football-field-sized ice slabs that shifted with the movement of the ocean. Every few hundred metres there would be churned-up ice rubble, like massive bags of popcorn, but my biggest threats were the open leads. This is where the ice had split through the strong undercurrent to expose the ocean, giving me a choice of either dropping into the ocean to cross it wearing an emersion suit, or taking a longer route to navigate around, deviating from my bearing. The latter was sometimes the most time-consuming, but also the safest. I used my ski poles to test some frozen leads to see if the ice was strong enough to hold my weight. I needed to remain practical with a clear head – the slightest mistake and it could have easily been fatal.

Snow had fallen over some patches, making them appear clear and smooth, but when I stepped on to it the jagged ice pushed through making the surface uneven. At one stage I unclipped my harness and left my pulk as I tested a route through the ice rubble, but I slipped and banged my head before lodging myself between the blocks of ice. As I lay still I did a mental check of my injuries before sitting up straight. I felt lucky to have made such a mistake but come through it. My location beacon and satellite phone were sitting in my pulk 15 feet away from where I lay. If the situation had been different, a small act like that could have had a serious impact on the expedition and my life. I needed to switch-on a bit more to get through this trip.

As my expedition had been cut short due to funding, I saw an opportunity for more filming and to become increasingly creative in how I filmed.

I would leave my pulk behind, taking only my essential survival kit in a small backpack and then weave my way through the ice rubble. I would line up a route of 50 to 100 metres and then on my way back to the pulk I placed *GoPro* cameras, switching them on to film my route back through with my pulk in tow. Then there would be a third trip to retrieve the cameras, but it was worth it to capture the moment.

I used a variety of views and perspectives for filming, with cameras on the back of the pulk and another on the front of my chest, as well as having remote cameras to film pitching the tent. I took distance shots to show the remoteness, combined with close-ups to allow me to do a piece to camera on the move. I would later edit these shots together with the support of my team back in the UK. Some of the most mundane situations, like cooking in my tent, recording daily satellite calls and mending my ever-breaking equipment became highlights within the film, *Solo Explorer*. People just wanted to understand what it was like to travel across the top of the world.

I kept the cameras wrapped in clear plastic bags to protect them from the ice and wind, and tucked them into my jacket to stop them from freezing. The bags also acted as a barrier for moisture – when stepping out of the cold into a tent that was being warmed by the cooker, there would be a distinct temperature difference that could affect the working parts of the camera.

The polar 24-hour light was excellent for capturing sharp pieces of film – everything stood out against the white canvas background, and colours especially. Oranges and greens that I wouldn't dare to wear in normal society seemed to work so well on film in this white environment.

My reason for filming so personally was to make the viewer feel that they were there with me.

On the fourth day I got up a little late and set off for a gruelling trudge, pulling my pulk through high ice rubble. It really struck me how great the contrast was between the Poles. In the South Pole I had been covering distances across expanses of open and rather flat plains which put very few obstacles in my path. Here in the North, I had rubble and thin ice to negotiate constantly, and instead of the dry environment of the South, at the end of each day everything was now damp.

I wore vapour barrier liners (thin sock-like bags) between my inner thin sock and my thicker outer sock to prevent sweat from passing through from my feet to the boot, but still my boots froze. It took a while to take off my boots at the end of the day, sat on the edge of my integral ground sheet, heaving my boots off with the little energy I had left. Once off, I treated my feet and dried them before putting on my 'night-time socks' and a light pair of 'camp booties', which are like down slippers with a hard sole so that I could go outside the tent if necessary. This routine would be the first act before I settled in for the night. My boots were then banged and thumped to remove as much ice as possible, and once I was satisfied I placed them in the corner of the tent vestibule for the morning's performance of putting them back on again. As previously mentioned, the smallest of mistakes can end an expedition. Tending to my feet in such a ritual way was one of the pieces of jigsaw for the success of the expedition.

The next day, with about 25 nautical miles to go, I was quite literally 'on thin ice'. Thankfully it was so cold that the ice was solid and was not too dangerous to walk on, just enough to hold my weight scurrying

On the move

across open leads. Sometimes I would unharness while I tested the thickness of the ice, in case I fell in – something that I had done in Antarctica as I carefully crossed crevasses that seemed to be full of solid snow. However, I never quite knew how packed it was, and if I was dragged down I didn't want the weight of the pulk pulling me further.

Crossing open frozen leads in the North, I made sure that all of my survival equipment was firmly attached to my body in waterproof bags, just in case everything went wrong. I could at least put up a shelter, make some food and a warm drink and then decide whether to make a satellite call or push my button on the emergency location beacon (ELB) to call for a rescue.

I managed to cross plenty of open leads without having to use an 'immersion suit' (which allowed me to enter the water without stripping off my clothes or boots). From the training in Canada with Richard Webber, I understood the hassle of taking the suit on and off. Richard had probably given me the best advice for this part of the expedition: the only way to reach the North Pole is to persist. Rather than spend the time entering the water, he had told me to find a way around it. He said that on his journey to the Pole he never once used his immersion suit – persist! How true this was, and I crossed many open leads of exposed water by taking the time to head around them instead.

Eventually I found myself on fairly flat ice and so I made some good progress. The temperature was bitter – the coldest I had experienced since 2003, when temperatures had been colder than -40°C (and in 2003 I had trained in darkness which had made the whole event even more stressful).

Skiing along I expected to warm up, but it just didn't happen. My body remained frozen, so I ended up with extra layers on to keep the chill out. It's surprising how much warmth can be gained from just wearing a thin extra covering. The terrain was a mixture of high ice followed by areas of flatness, and so my progress was equally as mixed. In two days I was due to reach the North Pole. The tendency would be to relax, but the creaking of the ice on top of the ocean reminded me how dangerous this situation was.

During that night I could clearly hear the currents of the ocean underneath the ice as I slept on it – a strange feeling, knowing that this was helping me edge closer to my final destination! The sound is pretty incredible, like being inside an old galleon ship with the creaking and thumping of the ocean against the wooden structure – a constant reminder of where I was, even with the tent zipped up and lying snugly in a sleeping bag. Some people have felt sea sick within their tents due to these sensations, and although I did not have this, it was still quite powerful.

In contrast, when the Arctic fell silent and I lay quiet in the tent, any sound outside was exacerbated. Strange noises could be heard and I had to distinguish whether they were outside or in my head.

On one occasion I heard a shuffle outside, like a crunch in the snow – in my head, a bear was approaching the tent. I got up two or three times, unzipped the door, and checked 360 degrees for signs, and saw nothing… but still the shuffling happened. I then realised that it was the sound of my breath over the hairs of my nostrils – the mind plays such strange tricks on you!

Safe in the warmth of my tent

The Expedition and Climate Change

During the final nights in the Arctic, I left my cooker on to heat up the tent because my body temperature had cooled right down – I knew the amount of fuel I had left and that I had the luxury to do this. I spoke with Dr Stephan Harrison, a climate change scientist who, as I've already mentioned, was also one of the patrons for the expedition. I had seen him last at the Royal Institute in London, just as I was about to start my solo to the South Pole. The Royal Institute is a charity dating from 1799, founded to introduce new technologies and teach sciences to the general public.

Dr Harrison works on fast climate change, specifically looking at landscape response to climate change over the past 20-30,000 years. Most of his work has been based in South America, and at this time he had just returned from a trip to the Californian desert looking into geomorphology in climate change.

During the call, which was also to be used on the website so that students could listen live, Dr Harrison explained how I had just travelled through two of the most important places in the world for understanding climate change. He explained how the Antarctic ice sheet controlled much of the rises in sea level which had been seen over the last century – and how it would continue to do so as we moved into the twenty-first century. He called it the 'elephant in the room', something which was becoming increasingly unstable because the sheet is losing enormous amounts of ice.

He continued to discuss how this had been predicted many years ago using planet modelling. The process is known as 'Arctic Amplification', and is caused by a range of feedbacks which kick in as ice melts, including one associated with changes to reflectivity. It was strange to listen to him as I thought about how warm I had felt on some days walking through the South Pole.

He explained that I was probably experiencing more open water than I had previously seen – which was of course true. He said that during the summer it was expected that the Arctic sea ice would reduce to almost zero, triggering all sorts of changes, and inevitably leading back to increased warming.

It was a sad conversation, but I felt that it was important to get the message out there, especially to all the children on the 'My Life in a Freezer' programme (the education programme we were conducting whilst I was out on ice). The effects of what I was seeing, although far from the experiences of most people, would one day impact their lives. We live in a world which is connected in many ways – socially, economically, politically and culturally – and therefore climate change will impact on the developing world, which will in turn impact the developed world – no one is immune to this reality.

Børge Ousland's wedding photograph (I'm far left)

On the final day of my twin Pole challenge, I started with just over twelve nautical miles to plough through. My progress was slow until I came to a large open area and I managed to push forward.

On Wednesday 11th April I reached the Geographic North Pole. When you reach the most extreme and remote area of the planet, you expect to feel an eerie silence, giving you time to soak in the solitude. This in fact was what I was craving for, complete isolation at the top of the world. However, when I reached the Geographic North Pole… there was a wedding taking place and I was about to gate-crash it!

Of all the things to do on a polar expedition, attending a wedding was not one that I had expected. The aforementioned Norwegian explorer Børge Ousland was getting married, and 20 or so people had been flown in via helicopter for the ceremony. I had seen fireworks go off 20 minutes before arriving at the Pole and had done a piece to camera saying, "I don't think these are for me."

To meet Børge for the first time at a place that I associate with him, especially in such personal circumstances, made me feel very proud. I was elated to be there and shared in the celebrations by drinking mulled wine. As far as we know, this was the first wedding ever to be held at this awesome location – on top of the world. Could this also be the biggest gate-crash in history? Out of everything I have been recognised for, this would be my favourite. I was even invited into the wedding photograph!

When the entourage was taken away by helicopter to continue their celebrations in Svalbard, I was left behind and had the Geographic North Pole all to myself. They had asked me if I wanted to go back with them but I said no. Once the helicopter had left I stood alone at last. I looked around and began to finally understand what a privilege it was to be there. As an ordinary person who comes from the centre of the UK, standing alone on top of the world I felt quite humble. I set up camp and spent the night there. It was a strange experience as I lay in my sleeping bag, thinking about the 6.8 billion people below me, with me literally 'on top of the world'. Over night the ice moved me 3.5 nautical miles away from the Geographic Pole, and again I was woken up several times by the rumbling of the ocean underneath me, reminding me that the expedition wasn't over, but I knew inside of me it was time to go home….

I spent the next few days pushing my way forward to Barneo Ice Station where the plane was to take me back to the mainland – practically south, but anything would have been south from the Pole. I arrived to a warm reception from my new-found friends, the Russians, who now had a different perspective about me as an explorer. What a way to have to prove yourself!

Alone at the Geographic North Pole

Anti-Climax?

Of course finishing any large project can often end with a feeling of anti-climax. If you spend months on ice, the idea of moving back into civilization and having all the comforts that we as humans take for granted – hot showers, watching a movie, eating a home cooked meal – may in fact not be as pleasurable and exciting as they would first appear, because these 'things' have become so insignificant during the expedition. I have the rest of my life to enjoy home comforts. For now I have created opportunities to experience the simplicities of life.

Heading back home was the realisation of coming back into the real world. Like most people, I have mixed feelings about our society. We have fantastic opportunities as humans to evolve in a unique, thought-provoking and creative way, but there is also an arrogance about human beings that I don't like – their neglect for the environment, animals and themselves upsets me. I have felt complete isolation in the cold extremes. It has made me grieve, smile, and laugh; it has given me a clear mind to reflect; and it has also allowed me to appreciate the spirituality of the world.

And as on this expedition, when I arrived at the end point, it was not a moment of triumph. For me it was an anti-climax because the journey had ended. Any expedition is really about the journey. Afterwards I tend to forget the bad parts very quickly, which of course enables me to plan another expedition. Speaking to a group of women, I once likened it to women having their second child – they quickly forget all the immense pain and horrors of the first birth.

Out on the ice, I had weeks of 'Zen-ness', where I felt completely at ease, which then carried on over for a few weeks into life post-expedition. So afterwards in normal life I felt that all my senses were more aligned; I felt so fit, energetic and younger. In this period it's as if nothing can faze me.

However, as the days and weeks pass, slowly the grain of life and the issues of just living get back into me – the bills, mundane problems to overcome, the niggles, the traffic – and that purity and simplicity starts to fade. And of course as this happens, I start to develop an itch to get back out there again, to find that isolation, and to escape the reality of life once more....

There's no sensation to compare with this
Suspended animation, a state of bliss
Can't keep my mind from the circling skies
Tongue-tied and twisted just an earth-bound misfit, I

Pink Floyd, 'Learning to Fly'.

The third pole of the planet, in my opinion, is Mount Everest. For me it is also a perfect platform to create an extreme classroom environment to engage with students from around the world.

People embark on expeditions for many different reasons. When faced with a potentially dangerous journey like Mount Everest, I need a reason for going there other than just for the glory of reaching the summit. I am inspired by what I see and feel in the extremes, so it is important for me to relay this back into classrooms that I link with, so that they too can experience the journey in their own extreme classroom.

Just after the North Pole expedition I found myself in the Himalayas, and as a polar explorer I was out of my depth, climbing mountains above 8,000 metres. I trained for three weeks on my own in the Nepalese side of the Himalayas with the idea of attempting an ascent of Mount Everest, but also, and most importantly, looking at new technologies to be able to bring 10,000 students along with me.

Again, Mark Kelly was involved in the beginning of the journey. He supported me in setting up an Inmarsat 'BGAN' unit, a very small device that used satellites to create a Wi-Fi space. With this I could then connect to the internet with an iPad. Once connected I could link to Skype and carry out a live visual call into schools – perfect! It was not quite so easy because Mark had to work hard to create the connection, racing against deadlines to reach each different school. We had arranged a date and time to conduct lessons in schools in countries such as Australia, America, the UK, Japan, Aland Islands, Thailand, Canada, Germany, Spain and others.

In the foothills of the Himalayas

As you would imagine, to do this we had to be spot on from our end, and on the other end there were over 200 students sitting in a sports hall with a massive screen on the wall, waiting for their explorers to appear. No pressure at all... but we managed each one and were able to engage with the students.

After a talk from the team about where we were, we would then receive some wonderful questions from the students – not always directed at me or Mark Kelly either. Sometimes it might be towards our official expedition photographer, Marc Pagani from New Orleans, or to Dr Pete Bradley my ascent partner from the UK. We wanted the students to feel part of the team, so we were honest on screen about how we felt, our worries and our hopes for the weeks ahead. I loved doing virtual hand shakes or fist bumps – high-fiving an explorer on Everest from your school in Thailand must have been a massive thrill for them all.

Four years after Everest I linked up with some of the directors who work for Microsoft / Skype to talk about new projects. Straight away one of them recalled a small boy from a school in the States that I had spoken to in the 'death zone' on the final ascent. I hadn't remembered him, as a lot had gone on in those final days. Apparently, he was an under-achiever who was reluctantly pushed towards the monitor to speak to me on Everest. After this he was so inspired that he changed his life around, worked hard at school and became a lot more sociable with his school friends – basically he became a better person. Another reason for me to explore.

In the course of 72 days of operating within the mountains, from the low valleys, through the schools, the villages, the monasteries, and moving up through the mountains where the trees disappear to the rocky areas, and finally to the glaciers, I linked up with the students. Once we began our ascent from Base Camp to Camps One, Two, Three, and Four, I then linked up with the schools again, although this time it was a lot more dangerous (for me).

As an example, one time I sat tied to an anchor at 7,500 metres up in the 'death zone', situated on the Lhotse Face. It's called the death zone as this is when your body is naturally closing down. You have limited time to operate within the two final camps to achieve the summit before you need to get down. It's also a pretty dangerous area to hold a lesson for 200 children!

As climbers using oxygen slowly passed me fighting their own battles, they would glance down at me through their goggles, sometimes doing a double-take to see whether they were hallucinating. I dropped my own oxygen mask so that I could speak to over 200 students in a sports hall in Australia. On my side was the harshness of the mountain and on theirs was a direct visual link to an explorer ascending Mount Everest. It was just so wonderful, and as I sit here writing this it makes me feel so proud. The expeditions are always secondary to these moments.

If anyone ever says that Mount Everest is easy to climb, then they haven't actually climbed it themselves. It is the hardest thing I have done, even including my military days and the solo trek to the South Pole.

Every step that I took above 6,000 metres was a deliberate thought. Above 7,500 metres, as you move into the death zone, your blood moves around your body like thick soup – oxygen is not getting to your brain quickly enough, your movements are slow, your judgement and thoughts are swayed, and you can feel sick. Your body has literally got limited time to survive, and whether you're an athlete or an ordinary person like me, you have roughly 48 hours to complete the final ascent.

Everest is a chess game, from Base Camp up to Camp One, Camp Two, and back to Base Camp for a five-day off-period to reacclimatise. Next you repeat that, but up to Camp Three, then back down for another five days of rest. After roughly 42 days you then do your final approach, which is Camp One, Two, Three, then to the saddle of Camp Four, just below 8,000 metres. This method was devised by great climbers of the nineties who paved the way so that people like myself could experience Everest for themselves.

There is of course a debate about whether this is ethical. You have to have had previous experience at high altitude to be on an ascent team, although this is sometimes over-looked. Generally, if a company runs an Everest expedition, they will insist their clients do a 6-7,000 metre peak with them as part of the package, which is a sensible idea.

I am often asked the question about the person who has so much money they are willing to pay their way to the top. My only answer to this is that it is down to the mountain guides to monitor the situation. For me, when I run polar or mountain treks, my main thought is getting everybody back alive. If that means making decisions that don't always sit well with the client, then so be it. A guide has an overall picture of events and the state of the team – this is a pure example of leading from the back, which I have mentioned previously.

I have read all of the negatives about Everest, but in the year I climbed the companies who ran the teams seemed to communicate well between them. Each team was allocated slots for their ascents, and there was little animosity. This allowed relative freedom for groups to move at their own pace, and so from this perspective I was impressed.

Welcoming visitors in the Khumbu region

Another point to note is that the mountain, along with other ventures in the area, brings in money to guides, local people, schools, villages and monasteries throughout the Khumbu region, all the way down and through Kathmandu. Tourism is the main income for their economy and acting responsibly seems to be a major priority.

However, regarding the issue of waste in various areas on the mountain, I was pretty disgusted. Base Camp wasn't too bad, as it was a lower level and a lot of waste was being taken back along the trekking routes and disposed of in the correct manner.

Camp One is a temporary camp and from what I could see it too was pretty clean. My shock came at Camps Two and Four, which are holding camps for teams resting between each significant height gain. These camps were unnecessarily filled with litter and human waste. Some teams tried their best to reduce this, but nobody could disrupt the reality of the situation. My team of four carried all our food and waste up and down the mountain (including oxygen bottles that I had paid extra for two porters to transport). This might sound like we went the extra mile, but the truth is that you can forget about extremely small and compact rubbish until you off-load it in the appropriate areas. Respecting the mountain, like the Poles, is essential to success.

Final Ascent

Like any typical man, I can never remember birthdays or significant dates, but I will always remember 19th May 2013. On this night, as I stood at just below 8,000 metres at Camp Four, I looked up to see a full moon lighting the shape of Mount Everest for our final ascent. It was -35°C with a 50 mph side-wind approaching from my left. In short, conditions were horrendous, but as a polar explorer I dismissed the pressures of the wind and the cold and focused on the semi-technical side of climbing a mountain. I kicked my crampons into the ice and hooked myself into the safety line, and as I looked up into the night sky I could see the summit of Mount Everest and the head torches of other climbers heading towards the summit. I leant back, breathed and relaxed my body to lower my heart rate, as I had taught myself on many long-range expeditions in the polar regions. I also felt that child inside me saying, "You're climbing Everest."

I started to ascend with the four-man team that we had put together ourselves. My good friend Singi Lama, who had previously climbed 6,000 metre peaks with me, took the lead. Singi had reached the summit on a previous occasion and it seemed like we were in good hands. Locked in behind me was Dr Peter Bradley, whom I had met a few years previously at a lecture I had given to his university in Liverpool, and behind him was our second Nepalese climber, Pemba Sherpa. I had never worked with Pemba before but he was 6'2" and had the frame of a rugby player, something unusual for the Nepalese. I felt like Pemba would be the one to grab me during the tough sections and haul me forward. As we ascended through the night, people passed us attached to the safety line on the way down with scared frozen faces saying, "Don't climb, don't climb."

However, we could see that we were fine. I knew that we were only a couple of hours from daylight breaking, when our bodies and minds would change as the sun gave us a surge of energy, so we pushed on.

At times I looked toward Singi, who would stop to re-adjust his karabiner on the line. I took it lightly to begin with, but after a while he was doing this with every tenth step and it put me mildly on edge.

In my rucksack, aside from the spare oxygen and some food and water, I was carrying an Inmarsat BGAN unit which would create the Wi-Fi space on the summit. With this we were going to create the first visual live-link to a film crew waiting in California with the head of the Microsoft/Skype merger team. No pressure there then!

Sometimes in life you need to assess the situation and make life-changing decisions…

Just 200 metres away from the summit, and after 72 days of being on that mountain with 10,000 students around the world following our every move, Singi dropped to his knees like a sack of potatoes. With the wind blowing up snow around us I approached him in the darkness and pulled him close to me. I shouted into his ear, trying to rise above the strong wind to ask if he was OK. At the same time I pushed his goggles up and looked into his eyes, but his eyes were all over the place. In the military and the rescue services I had seen people die in front of me, and I knew that at this moment, so close to the summit, Singi was closing down. He said he was OK, but his words were slurry and his movements were slow and weak.

I took a couple of steps back to Peter and told him that Singi was rapidly deteriorating. At that point Peter said that his own feet were frozen and that he needed to head back down to Camp Four. In my heart I knew that if everyone was OK, then Peter would have continued, as his blood just needed to flow and he was strong and had the will to continue – but we didn't have the luxury of time.

Pemba was next on my mind, and he had already started to descend the mountain. I demanded that he came back to our position, shouting at him through the wind – I was angry that he had just left his team with no reason. He appeared out of the darkness on his hands and knees. I could see tears and fear in his eyes. "I'm heading down now," he said, "I am heading down," and he kept saying this as we watched him disappear on the safety line. Then there were just the three of us….

Above the clouds

Each step on the ascent of Everest is a thought

The next decision I made was based on me as a human being, rather than as an explorer. I took one last look at the summit and the climbers' head-torches lined up towards it, and then turned back to the reality of the situation. I aborted the ascent. In truth I didn't think twice as Singi was dying. A life is worth more than planting a flag on top of a mountain.

We picked Singi up and carried him down part of the way until he could walk on his own. Then as a team we kept together and headed back to Camp Four. For almost two hours we pushed on through the wind, making sure we were in arm's length of each other, constantly encouraging Singi to move his feet and focus on the tents in the distance.

We walked into the devastation at Camp Four – tents had been blown away or torn apart in the night. I walked Singi to his tent and supported him into the warmth. We put him in his sleeping bag and made him some hot food and drinks. Pemba was with him (I didn't feel it was right to talk to Pemba at that point, as we were still in a dangerous area and would be for the next four days on the descent).

As I stepped back I tried to find my bearings as I focused my eyes on the colours and outlines of tents. Feeling emotionally drained and physically exhausted, I saw Pete and made my way to him. As I approached,

I could see he was taking a photograph of me coming out of the cold darkness with my oxygen mask fixed to my frozen face. My emotions were high and I shouted at him that this was not the time to take pictures – we had nearly lost one of our team mates. I let my anger loose on him and we both dropped exhausted into the tent. We lay in a heap for seconds that seemed like hours, and then breathed.

Having had a few minutes to reflect I turned to Pete and apologised for having a go at him. Looking back I had made a mistake to attack Pete, my friend and expedition colleague, especially as every great photograph is taken within the moment and Pete was only doing what had been asked of him… and more so. When I see this photograph now it always brings sadness into my heart as it transports me back to that night (see overleaf).

We rested for the night, and the next evening I considered doing the re-ascent, but if I am honest I only had 60% energy left in me – it was time to head down. People have asked me in talks since this event why didn't I solo to the summit, as I have had a lot of experience of operating alone. My reason was that I couldn't leave my friends in such a volatile area – if anything had happened to them, then facing their families or calling myself an explorer would always be difficult.

As we slowly ascended, the wind from above would whip up the loose snow to create a blast of icy particles in the air – like looking at the Milky Way

Pete's photograph of me in the night   *Approaching Camp Four on a saddle at 7,950m (26,085ft)*

Before leaving Camp Four I gave a live call to my team at Skype to inform them of what had happened and that we were safe and heading back down. After three days descending, all of the team, including Singi, Pemba and the porters, returned to the Base Camp safely. We all lived.

Every explorer in history has one thing in common. Whether it's great astronauts like Neil Armstrong, or leaders on the polar ice like Sir Ernest Shackleton, the fact remains that we are all story-tellers who have the shared responsibility to give an honest portrayal of what we have experienced. Sometimes people don't always make the decision we made. They feel that reaching the summit of a mountain or reaching the North or South Poles is the success of the expedition.

Yet for me the success of any expedition is to come back alive. If I had made a different decision that night at 8,500 metres, the past few years before writing this book would have been very different.

However, I was worried to see how the students would react to what I perceived at the time to be failure. Their response was truly incredible, and the honesty of how we had communicated the journey and the decisions made had a profound effect on the whole project. Reaching that point and turning back gave more life lessons than actually achieving the summit itself.

Other Expeditions

Due to this decision, I managed to go on with other great education programmes around the world, including crossing Iceland on foot with my highly entertaining and professional fellow adventurer Ryan Scarratt. We used a new method to pull equipment, called a MonoWalker. It had been designed by a German explorer called Kai Fuchs and was a single-wheeled trailer that strapped to a harness, allowing me to pull over 65 kilos by displacing the weight around my body instead of focusing it on my shoulders and back like a rucksack. It was a tremendous walk which was only dampened by the fact that it rained for 99% of the trip!

Aside from cycling solo across New Zealand, I also cycled across Oman with South / North Pole female veteran Ruth Storm and good friend Mark Kelly, thereby answering a question I get asked most of the time,

The Union Flag

Pause for thought during the descent of Everest

"Why don't you do warm places?" Our route from north to south Oman saw us swaying between camels, sleeping out in the desert, and swimming in the Arabian Sea – an expert in crossing Oman, Paul Graves, had been under strict instructions to ensure that I didn't overheat!

All of these smaller adventures were put together to support one of the University of Warwick's global educational initiatives, 'IGGY'. My role was to venture to these areas and deliver talks in schools *en route* and to also have an online presence on their own website that went out to over 16,000 students.

I later became Warwick University's 'Explorer in Residence', which is a bit amusing, but it was another area where I could relate from the extremes to a new audience of students, and it was also near my home town of Coventry – I felt honoured to be asked.

The truth is of course is that there is no journey. We are arriving and departing all at the same time.

David Bowie

North Pole Return – A Race Against Time?

I decided to write this book a few years ago. However, as I am pretty active in actually going on expeditions which take a lot of time to put together, I wasn't going to drop my passion to just write about it, and so during this period I found myself involved in another major expedition. I can only describe this one as a logistical nightmare mixed with very powerful results.

A return to the North Geographic Pole was planned by two other team members and myself whereby we would attempt to head to the Pole via the Canadian coastline.

Paul Vicary MSC is a Warrant Officer in the British Army – during his military career Paul faced many testing and hostile scenarios. Over the years, he has trained in extreme cold weather environments such as Norway, USA, Europe, Canada, Peruvian Andes and Antarctica. He is also a qualified army rock climbing instructor, mountain leader and ski tour instructor, not to mention a patrol medic and a state-registered paramedic.

During the winter of 2011/12, Paul completed a 920-mile unsupported journey following the route of Captain Scott to the Geographic South Pole, as part of the Centenary Race of Scott and Amundsen.

Our third team member was Mark Langridge MC, who recently retired from the army as a Warrant Officer after serving 27 years. As a qualified army instructor he has also experienced all climates including jungle, desert and polar. Mark completed a solo unsupported expedition to the South Pole in 2008/9, the same route that I had taken. He was also on the same centenary South Pole expedition as Paul, leading the Scott team.

Training at Warwickshire Golf and Country Club... as you do!

Both of the men were friends of the late Lt Colonel Henry Worsley, when they were part of the 2011/12 Centenary Expedition following Captain Scott's route to the South Pole; it was the same time as I reached the Pole during my solo journey.

As on this trip we were aiming to leave from the Canadian coastline, I immediately sent an email to the logistics flight company Ken Borak Air to arrange drop-off, safety coverage and pick up at the Pole.

Within days of contacting them we received a message saying that they were no longer operating planes on the ocean. In my world this was remarkable news. They had the most skilled pilots in the world who operated in such remote circumstances. However, the ice on the ocean was so unpredictable that they were reluctant to drop teams off – a fair point which immediately turned our attention to the Russian side of the ocean and a possible start point at Cape Arkticheskaya in Northern Siberia.

For nearly a year we negotiated with the Russians about fuel drops along the coastline, a point of entry and visas to enter Russia. During this period I was also busy bringing together the funding, the education package, the filming and the media support for the venture.

The communication with the Russians was very blunt at the best of times, and with each meeting I was becoming increasingly frustrated. In hindsight I was too emotionally attached to the expedition, so we needed to find a new approach to speed things up.

For the previous 18 months I had started to work with a wonderful woman, Suki Gallagher, who went from trying to support the idea for this book to basically managing my expeditions, speaking engagements and anything else that required support during the build-up. Suki has become a back-bone to the ventures and somebody I can discuss ideas with. A major area for her to focus on was speaking to our friends in Russia. Her calm but direct attitude saved the day on many occasions, and within a couple of weeks she had put the expedition back on track. If ever the British Government needed a negotiator, then Suki would be the one!

Within a month we were heading to Russia to begin the journey. However, the next issue came within days of securing the trip, when we were refused our team visa – with no explanation given. With Canada and Russia out of the frame, our expedition had failed before we had a chance to stand on the ice. It is still not clear why we didn't get the visas, but when we eventually stood 20 nautical miles from the Pole at Barneo, the holding camp, we discovered that there were 100 armed Russian paratroopers running an exercise at the Pole. If we had set off from the coast, then there was a fair chance we would have walked straight through their exercise (although this is just speculation)! Mark, Vic and myself would have only been armed with one gun, a pen flare and a pen knife… but I would have still fancied our chances! The result of this refusal of visas was that even though we had everything in place – such as funding, media and other requirements – we didn't actually have an expedition….

The balance of life is sometimes completely surreal.

As mentioned previously, in early 2016 Henry Worsley was evacuated from his solo attempt to cross Antarctica with only 30 nautical miles left to complete his epic challenge. He was airlifted to Punta Arenas in Chile where he later died in hospital due to complete organ failure. The news shocked the polar world, but the sadness ran deep with people who had experienced the privilege of playing small roles in his life.

I was asked to be interviewed on Breakfast TV and the BBC's *Newsnight* to outline the dangers of solo expeditions, and to say a little bit about Henry. I felt the world on my shoulders as I spoke live, with the knowledge that people who had known him for many years were probably watching – from long-time friends from the military who had served on operations with him, to his own family who were in mourning for their terrible loss.

Sitting wearing headphones in a dark booth in BBC Birmingham at 10.30 pm I stared into a small light. That was my view of the Newsnight programme – although the viewer at home could see the interviewer in a studio, a monitor showing my face which was superimposed against a backdrop of Birmingham at night, and side films of the Arctic. As a voice in my headphones told me that we had ten seconds until we were live, all I could think about was making sure I paid Henry the respect he deserved in front of his family and friends. I had never felt so much pressure than at that moment.

A day after the interview I received a heart-warming phone call from Steve Jones, the Base Camp manager in Antarctica for Antarctic Logistics & Expeditions. Steve, who had dealt with the whole process of Henry's death, thanked me for being respectful and honest. His parting words were, "If you or the team need anything then please let me know."

Vic shows his frustrations with the Russians

A waiting game

After chatting to both Mark and Vic, I called Steve up again the next day and asked him to vouch for our team's abilities to survive on extreme cold long-range journeys. He would speak to the Canadian logistics team to give them confidence in working with us on the North Pole attempt. Steve knew them very well because they had worked with him in Antarctica. Within a week they agreed on my new plan.

We were to do the North Pole in reverse. A Russian helicopter would take the three of us direct to the North Pole and then we would head south on ice to the Canadian coastline. As Plan C was put into play, it was left to Suki to go back to the Russians to confirm what we intended to do, for them to agree to drop our team off and to support our safety until 87 degrees south, at which time we would be supported by the Canadians. Suki succeeded in the negotiations and for the first time everybody was in agreement.

In a strange way Henry's parting gift to our team was to get us back out on expedition.

We headed to Svalbard to train and took Mark Kelly with us who operated a new drone that would film aerial shots of us training on the side of a glacier. It was great to have Mark back again in a supportive role. His insight into major expeditions was extremely valuable. A new team member who came along was photographer Denis O'Regan. His job was to capture the training, preparation and the build-up to the point of dropping us off at the North Pole.

Denis' photographic experience was really in music, having worked with big names like David Bowie, The Rolling Stones, Pink Floyd and many other legends. However, for now he had to

Onboard the helicopter crossing a frozen ocean

contend with three polar divas. At times he was slightly out of his depth – which was to be expected, especially when it came to working in minus temperatures – but having said that he took some great training pictures and in the evenings he would tell stories about his days with rock legends like Bob Marley, The Sex Pistols and Led Zeppelin. I truly respected Denis for stepping into this new arena. We train in tough areas, so he needed to learn quite quickly how to capture some great pictures.

Our time in Svalbard went from an expected one week to a frustrating three weeks. The problem was that the ice on the Arctic Ocean was depleting so much that the runway at Barneo, the temporary ice station, was constantly cracking. This cut into our valuable allocated time on ice and eventually Mark Kelly and Denis had to head home as we were still waiting for a slot to begin the expedition.

Each day all three of us remained active, keeping one ear to the ground to stay up-to-date about the state of the runway. We trained on a glacier at the back of our camp and alongside the town, heading along the coastline. We kept busy, but our frustrations were high.

With our ever-changing logistics, Vic came up with the phrase 'Plan D', which was to become our final option. The time allocated for the Canadians to pick us up in safety had now gone, so our attempt for the coastline was no more. The only option we had left was to do the last two degrees to the Pole. This meant a two-week push on ice, and so before making a decision we re-addressed our mission statement for the expedition.

The aim was to film an honest account of our journey across the Arctic Ocean to show how difficult it is to complete this in the modern era. The story was already there before we had even boarded the helicopter – environmental damage had prevented a coastal attempt. Mother nature had reduced our journey, which was not only damaging for the actual adventure, but more significantly it was devastating for the damage to the Arctic Ocean caused directly by climate change.

We finally flew into Barneo and within an hour of briefings and fuelling cookers, the Russian long-range helicopter flew us a further 150 miles out on the ocean, south towards Russia. Even at this stage my frustration grew as the pilots refused to drop our team in the area we wanted because it was too dangerous – instead they wanted to drop us closer to the Pole. Without Suki there to fight our corner, I demanded they land. We were experienced and at this point we just wanted to get on with it! A familiar feeling.

The helicopter dropped us on ice and after a few hours' sleep we packed up and set our bearings north. After all of the issues we had faced over three years we now had two weeks to document our approach to the Pole.

After a relaxed start we went on to experience open sections of water the size of football pitches, ice rubble the size of double-decker buses and open leads that would take us on long detours to try and maintain our bearing. We filmed these crossings using impartial views which focused on the team members so that the viewer could relate to us and so hopefully understand the hostile area we were crossing.

We reached the Geographic North Pole (GNP), but unlike before there was no wedding reception. This time we felt the remoteness and the strength of how global warming had made expeditions like this almost impossible to complete. I would go to the extent of saying that we might have even seen the last coastal expeditions to the GNP – which is a devastating environmental statement to make.

The expedition documentary was called 'A Race Against Time'. We were the only team in the world in 2016 to operate so remotely on the Arctic Ocean in the warmest season ever recorded at the GNP. The documentary covers not only the journey, but also the impact humans are having on our planet – neglect caused by the ignorance and greed of humanity. It is all well and good creating strong films and having damaging evidence, but you then need an audience to watch them. My past solo films had been supported by my good friend Ryan Scarrett (my Iceland crossing partner) and screened by his then company Information TV on the Showcase Channel, which has a wide-reaching audience.

Training in the Longyearbyen Glacier

If a documentary is current to global news then it sometimes just keeps developing and changes direction. We arrived back from the North Pole armed with great footage and recruited director, writer and film-maker, Steve Reynolds, a close friend from my home town of Coventry. In 2008 Steve had travelled to Alaska with me to shoot a short set of documentaries for schools on the relationship between Alaskan mushers and their dogs.

This was a mini-venture I had set up to deliver for free to over 60 schools in the UK. Steve and myself became good friends out of it and he went on to develop some Hollywood and UK films. Luckily he gave his time to edit and support post-production, as well as a first draft for the script on the documentary.

Pick-up at the North Pole

Myself, Mark Langridge and Paul Vicary at Heathrow

Through a good source we had met within the film industry we managed to link up with British actor Tom Hardy who was generous in giving up his free time to add the voice-over to the film. Tom is a true gentleman and a pure professional. It felt so surreal listening to him narrate the documentary as we sat in his house in London. At one point he had finished part of the voice-over and looked at Steve and myself to ask, "Is it ok?" Steve said, "That's perfect," and I said it was good, but asked if he could do it in his Bane Voice (the villain he played in director Christopher Nolan's Batman film, *The Dark Knight Rises*). I instantly thought, "What the hell have I just said?" but straight away Tom did the piece again in the dark evil voice of Bane!

Having Tom's (real) voice added to the film gave it a remarkable edge. Tom's dad, Chips, also supported in co-writing the script with Steve. Having these people involved was crucial to gaining a wider audience so that our footsteps on ice had real significance.

However, as the film expanded we began to realise the potential of what we were doing. I started thinking about how to expose what I was experiencing to a wider audience and here we were with crucial footage in an era of global climate change. I was introduced to an award-winning documentary film maker Tom Martienssen from a friend in the BBC called Russ Inman.

Over the next two years Tom and myself filmed in the Himalayas on Everest, working with anti-poaching teams in Africa. In contrast to this we then filmed again in the cold of Alaska with dog teams and later in schools in New York and New Jersey. We edged the narrative of the film towards how contemporary explorers operate in this modern era of climate change. As you would have read from this book, the struggle to form an expedition is sometimes just as challenging as heading out into the void, so with this we focused on the explorer as well as the environment. Two award-winning production companies are onboard and the journey continues to make something that is relevant and causes the viewer to think about their own responsibility towards the planet.

The North Pole expedition finished on ice but the legacy continues...

*Live everyday like it's your last
and someday you'll be right.*
Woody Allen

146

In the End

Having read this book, you will know that it hasn't just been about about telling stories of journeys in a freezer or 'swinging the lamp', as we used to say in the Fire and Rescue Service. I hope the reasons why I explore and what drives me to give up everything in life to follow my passion has come across.

From the moment that I understood how to survive within the cold extremes of the planet I began a journey to learn my trade. In the beginning it was based on a feeling of freedom – walking in remote areas where very few humans had walked before. From working with indigenous people and guiding different teams I then went on to understand the importance of the environment and the impact we have as humans towards our planet – our home.

A reason to explore always bugged me – if I didn't have one then I was just a 'professional camper'. So I started to develop education programmes that now attract millions of students around the world. I have learnt how to film and photograph so that people can see and understand the reason for modern day exploration, and I have developed my own style of leadership. My first expedition was linked to one classroom in my old school, Finham Park Comprehensive, and my last expedition linked to over 1.2 million students worldwide.

Remembering my first adventure as a child where I risked everything to reach the local sweet shop in Coventry, I feel seeds were planted which led me in later life to plan major expeditions around the world, standing shoulder-to-shoulder with some of the best explorers in the business. However, I am still learning – and the hunger is still there. My mantra is to act like a contender and never a champion. This keeps me grounded and focused.

As a six-year-old boy I was curious to see what was around the next corner. Today I still feel the same, whether it's walking my dogs on a new route from my green English village, or climbing through the clouds into a white void on Mount Everest.

Some say that life in itself is indeed an adventure, whether it's following in the footprints of ghosts, or creating new exciting ideas for future exploration.

Full Circle

The opening photograph in this book is a picture taken by Apollo 8 astronaut William Anders who, in 1968, was part of the first manned mission to orbit the moon. They saw the earth in its purity as they re-appeared

from the dark side of the moon, and at that point Anders took the iconic picture called Earth Rise. He went on to say about that moment, "We set out to explore the moon, and instead discovered earth."

The irony is as this book is being published we are celebrating 50 years since the first moon landings of Apollo 11. I have had the honour of becoming an ambassador to astronaut Buzz Aldrin's eduction programme 'The Peoples Moon' and asked Aldrin's manager how Michael Collins feels about being known as the most remote human being in the history. Collins understands the idea but prefers to be remembered for being part of 'the team' that brought the first men on the moon back to earth safely.

So the act of being alone is only part of the story – it's what you do and how you explore that can make a real difference.

Acknowledgements

This book is called *SOLO Explorer*, a strange title given the amount of people below who have gone above and beyond to make my expeditions a reality. Without these people believing in me my expeditions and education programmes would never have happened.

To the following who believed in me first and then my reason to explore:

Paul and Lisa Baker, Jon and Emma Sharp, George Herd, Gordon Richardson, Dr Mark Smith, The Drayson Foundation and the teams at Skype in the Classroom, Engine Lease Finance, Grant Thornton, Virgin Money, McCann's Manchester.

Thank you to the following people for supporting the operational side of the expeditions:

Mark Kelly, Ryan Scarratt, Jon Geldart, Marc Pagani, Ruth Storm, Paul 'Vic' Vicary, Tom Martienssen, Krishna Magar, Devendra Rai, Mauli Rai,.

Thank you to the following who have supported the logistical side of running an exploration company:

Suki Gallagher, Alistair Richards, Zakia Rashi, Rob Ford, Tony Gray, Dr Phil McTernan, Steve Boreham, Russ Inman, Gerry Hill, Dr Harbinder Sandu, Dr Stephan Harrison, Denis O'Regan, Nigel Byde, Simon Riley, Grant Dudson, Steve Jones, Si and AJ, Tom Hardy, John 'the' Brush, Carlos Burgos, Joe Latham.

Thank you to these great organisations for their support:

Suunto, Salomon, Printworks Coventry, Grant Thornton, Jupiter Marketing, Farmfoods, Coventry Rugby Club, Contact Engine, Apache Brave, The University of Warwick, The Warwickshire Golf and Country Club, Spirit of George.

Charities and support groups:

Hire A Hero UK, The Princes Trust, Children's University, Sporting Equals, The International Scouting Movement, Dog Sled Therapy UK, The Monday Club Coventry, Sherbourne Fields School, Finham Park School, Stivichall Junior School, The Explorers Club – The Great Britain and Ireland Chapter, The Royal Geographic Society.

Thank you to my family and friends for their support and patience:

Rob, Gris, Emily and Sam, Dad and Charlie (dog); Alex Hatfield, Rory Golden, Malcolm Glen, Glen Raynor.

...and my kids, Ceara and Pop – for giving me a reason to return home.